NEW *Paradigm*

BOOK 1

Awakening the Journey Within

---✸---

Guidance for Personal
and Generational Transformation

MICHELE KETZMERICK, MARY KRAMER,
and the legacy of VINCE KRAMER

Copyright © 2025 by Mary Kramer

New Paradigm
Awakening the Journey Within
Book 1

All rights reserved.

No part of this work may be used or reproduced, transmitted, stored, or used in any form or by any means graphic, electronic, or mechanical, including but not limited to photocopying, recording, scanning, digitizing, taping, Web distribution, information networks or information storage and retrieval systems, or in any manner whatsoever without prior written permission from the publisher.

In this world of digital information and rapidly-changing technology, some citations do not provide exact page numbers or credit the original source. We regret any errors, which are a result of the ease with which we consume information.

Without in any way limiting the author's and publisher's exclusive rights under copyright, any use of this publication to train generative artificial intelligence (AI) or Large Language Model (LLM) technologies to generate text is expressly prohibited.

This book reflects the author's present recollections of experiences over time. Some names and characteristics have been changed, some events have been compressed, and some dialogue has been recreated.

Edited by Laurie Knight
Cover Design by: Kristina Edstrom

An Imprint for GracePoint Publishing (www.GracePointPublishing.com)

GracePoint Matrix, LLC
624 S. Cascade Ave, Suite 201, Colorado Springs, CO 80903
www.GracePointMatrix.com
Email: Admin@GracePointMatrix.com

SAN # 991-6032

A Library of Congress Control Number has been requested and is pending.

ISBN: (Paperback) 978-1-966346-22-7
eISBN: 978-1-966346-23-4

Books may be purchased for educational, business, or sales promotional use.
For distribution queries contact Sales@IPGbook.com
For non-retail bulk order requests contact Orders@GracePointPublishing.com

Printed in U.S.A

Table of Contents

Foreword v
A Note Before We Begin ix
Introduction 1
Letter to the Readers 5
Guides 9
Receiving Guidance 19
Obstacles 27
Purpose 35
Resistance 45
New Paradigm 55
Expansion 65
Divine Intent 71
Not Believing 81
Believing 89
Roadblocks 97
Meant for More 105
Chaos Explained 115
Trust 125
Separateness 133
Higher Self 141

Reason on Earth	149
Earth Transformation	157
Navigating the World	165
Universal Knowledge	175
Either/Or	185
Gratitude	193
Supporting the Children	203
Next Steps	211
Death	217
Epilogue	225
A Note from Mary	229
About the Authors	231

Foreword

In 2001 I was ranked as one of the world's top fifty psychics. I even had my brain examined by scientists at the University of Arizona in Tucson. I also worked at a walk-in New Age center in Sedona, Arizona and made my living as a spiritual guide.

In spite of all of this, I seriously doubted my intuitive abilities.

I felt like I could tune in easily to other people's energies and give them guidance, but frankly, I chalked up my ability to "psychically divine" for others as just a result of my training as a nurse. When it came down to me feeling spiritually connected and supported, I was lost.

There is a moment on the spiritual path when everything that once felt certain begins to tremble. Your worldview shifts, your sense of identity crumbles, and you begin to question what's real, what's meaningful, and why you're here. If you're holding this book, chances are you've felt that tremble—or maybe you're deep in it. And if you're anything like most of us, you've also encountered one of the least talked about, but most persistent, obstacles along the way: self-doubt.

This book, which holds the teachings of the late Vince Kramer, is not just another guide to spiritual awakening. It is an honest, deeply personal, and profoundly practical offering for anyone who is waking up to the truth of who they are—and wrestling with the resistance that inevitably rises. At its heart, this is a book about remembering: remembering your purpose, your power and your connection to something greater. But just as importantly, it is a book about the struggle to believe in that remembrance when everything in your conditioned mind tells you otherwise.

The wisdom of Vince's teaching is balanced by the honesty of Michele, who busts the romantic myths of walking a spiritual path with the intimate sharing of her own struggle to connect spiritually in spite of putting forth a great deal of effort.

Spiritual awakening is often romanticized. We hear stories of sudden enlightenment, divine downloads, and euphoric moments of clarity. And yes, those experiences exist—but what we don't hear enough about is the grit or the aching vulnerability. The days when everything feels like a lie. The voice in your head that whispers, "Who do you think you are?" That voice is self-doubt, and it's the shadow side of awakening that few talk about—and even fewer prepare us to face.

Self-doubt isn't just a passing thought. It's a deeply embedded belief system, built over years—lifetimes even—of conditioning. It's the internalized voice of teachers, parents, systems, and experiences that told us not to trust our intuition, not to dream too big, not to stray too far from the norm. When we begin to wake up spiritually, these voices don't just disappear. In fact, they often get louder, more insistent, because the ego senses it's losing control. And in the noise of that inner resistance, many people quietly abandon their awakening, believing the lie that they're not "ready," "worthy," or "spiritual enough."

Mary and Vince Kramer understood this intimately—not just as spiritual teachers, but as fellow travelers on the path. They lived this journey. They stumbled; they doubted; they faced loss, grief, uncertainty—and kept going. What they discovered, and what they now offer to you through this book, is that self-doubt isn't something you conquer by force or bypass with positivity. Instead, it is something you meet with honesty, curiosity, and love.

One of the things that makes this book so powerful is its refusal to pretend. It doesn't hide behind lofty metaphors or bypass the messiness of growth. Mary, Michele, and Vince write from experience with humility, compassion, and the kind of grounded wisdom that only comes from walking through the fire. This wisdom, married with the deep teachings of The Round Table, gives you a systematic journey to your personal spiritual awakening.

Vince, who has since passed on from the physical world, brings through in these pages not just his human voice, but also channeled messages from a higher source—messages that transcend time, death, and the boundaries of the material world. His presence in this book is both subtle and profound. It reminds us that even when someone we love passes on, their wisdom, energy, and love remain with us. And in that, there is healing.

Mary carries this torch with clarity and grace. She reminds us that awakening isn't about perfection. It's about devotion. It's about showing up for your truth again and again, even when you're scared, even when you're uncertain, even when your knees are shaking.

So, what do we do with self-doubt? How do we move forward when we're unsure of who we are, let alone where we're going?

This book doesn't offer easy answers—but it does offer real ones, coupled with easy-to-follow instructions and contemplations that will give you a way forward and a path to connect to your Higher Self.

Through their stories, teachings, and channeled insights, Mary and Vince illuminate a path forward—not as gurus, but as guides. They help us understand that doubt is not an enemy, but a doorway and that purpose is not something you find "out there," but something you remember from within. They reinforce that the spiritual path is not a straight line, but a spiraling journey back to your own heart.

They also remind us that you are not alone. Not now. Not ever.

That's one of the most quietly revolutionary aspects of this book. It doesn't just hand you tools or theories—it invites you into a relationship with the wisdom inside you—with Spirit, with the unseen world that surrounds and supports you. And perhaps most importantly, with a community of others who are walking through the same fire, asking the same questions, facing the same fears.

We're living in a time of massive transition. The old ways are crumbling. The systems that once gave us a sense of identity and purpose are no longer sustainable. More and more people are waking up to a deeper truth—that they are more than what they were taught to believe, that they came here with a purpose, and that they are connected to something far greater than themselves.

But awakening in this world is not easy. It takes courage to say, "I want more. I want truth. I want to live aligned with my soul."

And it takes support—real support—to keep going when everything inside you says, "Maybe this is all a mistake."

That's what this book offers: not just knowledge, but support. Not just ideas, but clear instructions to help you stay connected to the true story of who you are and who you were meant to be in this lifetime. It is a lighthouse for the spiritually curious and the spiritually committed alike.

And most of all, it is a reminder that you are not broken for doubting yourself, because that doubt can be a sacred threshold. It reminds us that awakening is not about being fearless—it's about moving forward with your heart open, even when you're afraid.

As you turn the pages of this book, I invite you to do so slowly. Let it wash over you. Let the stories, the teachings, and the channeled messages speak to the quiet places inside you: the places that ache, the places that hope, and the places that are ready to remember.

Let Mary and Vince's work and Michele's honest sharing be more than ideas—let them be catalysts.

Let them remind you that your path, no matter how winding or unclear, is valid, that your doubt does not disqualify you, that your questions are holy, and that the very fact you are asking them means you are already awakening.

Thank you, Vince, for this powerful legacy of teachings. Thank you for sharing your Heart in the physical and the nonphysical world.

From my Heart to Yours,

Dr. Karen Parker

A Note Before We Begin

As you embark on this journey through the pages of this book, I want to take a moment to introduce you to someone who has been instrumental in bringing this work to life. Michele has been not only a cherished friend but also a true partner in the creation of this book. Her insights, dedication, and understanding of Vince's teachings have added a depth and richness to the work that I know you will feel as you read.

Michele's introduction and letter to you, the readers, is not just a prelude to the content that follows; it's an invitation to open your heart and mind to the profound wisdom and transformative ideas that this book offers. Her words carry the essence of our shared journey, and her perspective will guide you as you step into the new paradigm that Vince so passionately believed in.

Michele was there with Vince in the final hours before his passing, working closely with him to complete the writings you are about to immerse yourself in. Her bond with Vince and her unwavering commitment to this project in the face of sudden loss are testaments to the deep trust and connection that defined their collaboration. The emotions she conveys and the insights she shares are not just reflections of Vince's teachings—they are the raw and honest expressions of someone who has been profoundly changed by them.

As you read Michele's introduction and letter, I hope you feel the same sense of connection, inspiration, and readiness to explore that she felt while writing them. This book is a co-creation in every sense of the word, and Michele's voice is a vital part of that creation. Her words are a reminder that we are all in this together, learning, growing, and expanding our understanding of the world and ourselves.

Thank you for being here, and for being open to what lies ahead.

With love and appreciation,

Mary

Introduction

It was late into the evening of June 11, 2024. Final texts were sent, and I was completing the edits of these writings you are about to immerse yourself in. The following morning, I was on the road when the call came.

"Vince died this morning."

Mary's words were clear, almost calm. Shock does strange things to our psyches. When I had answered hello to Mary, cell coverage was poor. I heard her say, "Michele, I have the greatest news." But what she actually said was "I have devastating news." And she did.

Mary was at the Dallas airport waiting to board a flight to the home where her husband had died suddenly. She shared briefly what she knew so far, and then, with an intensity of tone and focus: "Please get the book out. We have to get the book out. It is very important. It has to get out."

I assured her that I would do whatever necessary to assist with the process. My thoughts were reeling! I could not believe Vince was gone. We had completed editing our final chapters the evening prior, only hours before he died. My heart broke open for Mary, their families, their community, and our beautiful Purpose Meaning Joy community. However, with the trust that had developed and grown for Vince and Mary, for my own newly chosen trust in myself, and the writings we created together, I knew my commitment to completion would not waver.

Although the meat of the writing was finished, there was one part left for Vince to complete, this introduction. It is difficult not to cry as I write this only days after, and it may sound odd to some to have developed this strong and powerful friendship across countries, over Zoom. But it is a friendship where I have been fortunate to experience meaningful growth, support, and the gentle guidance of Vince and Mary, and the extraordinary coaching and powerfully clear channel that was my friend and coach, Vince Kramer. The messages feel more elevated now that they are being shared on behalf of and in honor of Vince, posthumously. It is my intention and hope that through the nonphysical, high frequency messages and the translated everyday experiences, that a similar transformation unfolds for you, in whatever ways benefit your very highest good.

Vince's purpose on Earth and the very existence of humanity are revealed for all of us through the channeled messages herein. They serve as a beacon as we move into the new paradigm, whether we see it, believe it, understand it, or not. Remaining unchanged once you wholeheartedly immerse your inner self in the high frequency messages shared with the world at this anticipated time would be challenging to say the least. You now have access, through immersing yourself in this book, to further understand why you are here, why you chose this life, and the deeper meaning of *everything*. If reading a book was ever an adventure, it is in this writing, the holy grail of the purpose of existence. The most significant questions are answered through the clear channel of a gifted and brilliant man. Vince's process for accessing high frequency information was Active Connection; he tuned into the energy of his nonphysical Trusted Source, asked questions related to the new paradigm, and transcribed the responses.

You are now privy to the answers to life's most significant queries from the highest frequency source of guidance, and with it, you will discover your own deepest reasons for being here, in this physical body, at this time. It is with heaviness and excitement bubbling in the same pot, and especially with great appreciation and affection for my dear friends Mary and Vince, that I share this introduction. The following pages include guidance and stories of a journey into the doorway of the new paradigm. It is a loving invitation extended to your open mind and your beautiful, expanding heart.

Letter to the Readers

I was aware that the waking-up experience is not the same for everyone, even though I was never really sure what waking up meant. I was very aware that in my everyday, physical life, I am a slow riser; each morning, it's a gradual wake up, especially since retirement. Before retirement, my routine involved hitting the snooze button several times, usually without conscious awareness. With retirement, after a few deep breaths and cat stretches, my mind chases me out of bed with thoughts of the day ahead, sometimes the day before, sometimes with worries about loved ones and my health, and often, self-deprecating thoughts about how horrible I ate the previous day, followed with a plan to do at least a little better with a new day.

In my limited experiences of the nonphysical, or seeing the world and everything in it as energy, my process of waking up in that sense was taking a similar trajectory, especially as I hit the proverbial snooze button many times over the decades—until recently.

I was taken by complete surprise when I was invited to collaborate on this writing project. After my career, I was so *done*! I was depleted, ready to do nothing except fun stuff, and I felt my purpose in this life was complete! I was in my late fifties and grateful and ready to rest for the remainder of my days. The fun stuff that I had looked forward to was related to a deep curiosity about some very important existential questions, *the most important questions.* Are we here to work most of our lives, do the laundry, pay the bills, then die? Coincidently, this anticipated post-career respite occurred during the COVID-19 era: no travel, no connecting, too much isolation. This forced isolation was spent with my ADHD spouse; otherwise, it might have equated to well-deserved solitude. But I did have loads of time to continue a search that was, up to this point, limited by my work life and family responsibilities.

Vince and Mary's work came near the end of a lengthy expenditure of time, energy, and cash, turning over every metaphysical and mystical rock that my hungry mind could find. It was a relentless search for certainty, hopefully finally revealing a collective or at least somewhat agreed upon truth about why we are here, what happens when we die, and if we have a larger purpose. *Is it a must?* The search was always for answers *outside* of myself.

Having nothing to lose, I signed up for their free Your Life, Your Way session. The conversation with Vince and Mary drew me in, in an interesting and authentic way. In my turning-over-every-rock phase, I experienced numerous modalities, with *many* mediums, intuitives, and channelers (highlights to be shared later in the book). At the time of the session, I thought it was worth another try, to maybe hear something I had not thought of, something that would lead me closer to proof that the nonphysical was real, or something different from the others I'd studied and read. Plus, there was the joy of more free stuff! I started tuning in with a burning question for every monthly freebie with The Round Table, the nonphysical energies Vince connected with. I was as intrigued as I was with the others, expecting that soon, the next shiny thing would squirrel me in another exciting direction. I read their book and enjoyed an extraordinary story of wake-up calls. Soon after, I felt compelled by what I had learned so far, to sign up for a short course. With more time and connection with both Vince and Mary, I felt their sincerity, dedication, and conviction in their work. And I resonated with what I had previously thought was rocky at best, the marriage of science and the nonphysical. The Round Table communicated logically and in a refreshing, forward manner relevant to living day-to-day life. Yes, another channeler, but seemingly relevant and different from others I had experienced. At an early glance, this seemed to me unlike your run-of-the-mill New Age shenanigans.

This was the time, I realized, to step into the fullness of the life I planned—no more snooze button. That sentence may make a little more sense within the context of the following pages. I look forward to sharing when and how I realized that there was so much more than what I had been taught and believed throughout my life. How excited and honored I felt when asked by higher vibrational energy through Vince and Mary to share my interpretation of nonphysical messages and answers received by Vince. It is my intention and sincere hope that you find in my stories nuggets of relevance and the often-elusive answers to your curiosities and larger questions. I invite you, dear readers, to experience the following pages with an open mind and an open heart. I am humbled and grateful for you and for this opportunity.

Michele

Guides
(AC—Active Connection—10 Jan 24)

All the knowledge of the Universe is available to you at all times. When you tap into the guidance available to you at the higher vibrations, you are connecting with what you might call your guides. These guides are available to you wherever and whenever to support you on your chosen journey.

The Round Table, channeled by Vince Kramer

Vince's Question: Good morning. I think there is a question that is necessary for those who doubt Active Connection, maybe even meditation or prayer and connecting with guidance. Can you share who you are or who we can connect with when we say we talk with our guides?

> **Trusted Source's Response:** This is a very good question, and yes, the answer can be very helpful to many. You have shared about separation or separateness before, and receiving guidance can be a place where many fall into the belief that the guidance is coming from outside of them instead of part of the Universal Energy that they are.

Yes, I know what you mean. It is easy to believe that we are lesser than or subservient to these guides. Will you explain in a way we can easily understand?

> There is one true energy, and it is called many things by you: God, Source, Universe, and there are many more, and there are strands or streams of this energy that make up the whole. There are twelve main strands of this energy. You have seen references to the twelve in many different ways. Some are the rays of light or the twelve tribes. There is more of this we can explain at another time. Each strand and every combination of the strands are represented by humans on your planet.
>
> As we share this with you, know that we use "energy strands" and "energy streams" interchangeably. Let us give you an example of what we are saying. Let's say there is a human on your Earth named Bob. Bob chose to represent the energy stream which is represented by the color blue. As a human being, Bob is the lower frequency of that energy stream. In the lower frequencies, Bob remembers very little of the all-knowingness of Universal Energy.
>
> There are unlimited frequencies of the blue energy stream. Bob's Higher Self, the nonphysical part of Bob, is a higher frequency than the physical third-dimensional part of Bob. Therefore, the nonphysical at the higher frequency can access, remember, and understand a greater amount and level of this divine knowledge. As you move up the vibration of the energy stream at the higher frequencies, even more can be accessed, remembered, and understood.
>
> These higher frequencies are what you call your guides. Because these guides are part of your energy stream, they are easily accessed to help you understand or see the answers to the questions you might have. Also, each energy stream or combination of energy streams has a specific purpose. This means that the higher frequencies, your guides, also share your purpose and can assist you with help and guidance for you all to live your chosen purposes on Earth.

That is very advanced and challenging to accept. How can you make it simpler?

> You all are part of the whole. You are Universal Energy. The higher frequencies of the energy you choose to represent are available to help you access the information you desire to live fully the reason you chose to come to Earth.

That was helpful and a little easier to understand. Why do we connect to the Archangels and the Ascended Masters when we ask for guidance?

> It is more satisfying to the human mind. Each of the angels and masters are also frequencies of the energy streams; as such, they, as the higher frequencies, have access to the highest levels of knowledge and understanding. If you look at Bob again, Bob's energy stream is represented by the color blue. There are many angels and masters also representing that stream. In the case of the blue energy stream, Archangel Michael is the highest vibration of the stream.
>
> Being able to put a name on these higher frequencies satisfies the human mind. This explains why you may feel drawn to certain masters and angels. This knowingness will help you get the answers you seek. Tap into the knowledge that will best serve you in living the life you were meant to live and best deliver the gifts and talents that are uniquely you. We at the higher frequencies are here to assist you in expanding the frequencies of the source energy.
>
> Our Divine Intent is to support all of you, for we are all one.
>
> In this now, Namaste.

Namaste.

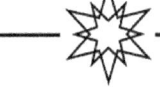

Michele's Musings

The question about doubting Active Connection certainly resonated with me! I was limited in my understanding because my experience of connecting is limited and, as of yet, not easy for me to attain or trust. I was enjoying these transmissions from Vince's guides, especially because of my natural inclination to seek answers outside of myself. I was still grappling with guides as a concept because I had never experienced what I would consider a *real* connection with a guide. Despite numerous courses and attempts to connect with one, I honestly did not have certainty that I actually had one.

This Active Connection about guides clarified the energy streams and how I should be able to connect with the guides in my energy streams easily, but it was not yet convincing or experienced as a felt sense. Even after being told about my specific energy streams (more about that later), I still found it challenging, and when I attempted tuning into guidance via Active Connection, I regularly questioned whether it was my imagination.

Early on, I had many questions. Are guides *only* angels? Are angels not normally associated with religious beliefs? Generally speaking, I had released religious dogma some time ago. So, who are they? *What* are they? How do we know they are communicating? At one time, I had requested proof of the existence of nonphysical helpers by way of a handsome angel at the foot of my bed or, as a little more edgy attempt, a near-death experience with guides, past loved ones, and life-altering love hugs from the other side.

I admit I wanted the big stuff. I *needed* the big stuff! The visible angel, lucid dreams, astral travel, hearing from deceased loved ones, or just chatting with a trusted nonphysical guide. I read about it all; I researched numerous books about it, and I wanted to be able to do it all on demand. But what if I was one of the many humans who could never do it? I was stubborn, though, like the little engine that could. Here are a few examples of my efforts.

I had settled into a deep state of relaxation in my sunroom. I followed the instructions carefully, breathing while listening to the YouTube meditation lulling in my headphones. I felt relaxed, like I was dozing in and out. I was using the recommended affirmations, waiting to feel myself sink into a deeper and deeper state, the state that can induce the ultimate—an out-of-body experience. I was conscious of the music and then no longer conscious of music. Then, I was suddenly jolted awake when Cooper, my little Lhasa apso, jumped up onto the chair near mine. I settled into a relaxed state again, but within minutes, he dropped his chewie on the hardwood floor, and I was startled into a fully awake and somewhat annoyed state.

Weeks later during another attempt while relaxing on my bed, feeling myself settle into a deep, relaxed state, suddenly, I sensed through closed eyelids the room lighting up in a warm glow. My heart sped up; *it was finally happening!* Then I felt the familiar furry paws scratching at the side of the bed near my head. It was Cooper again! He had pushed the door open with his little black nose, flooding the room with sunlight. He just missed me and wanted snuggles. *Maybe he was my guide?*

The attraction to astral traveling? I read a book written by a local author who found his guides this way. So, I tried astral projection in a serious (and expensive) way: a six-day course on Vancouver Island. It was a beautiful, sunny, spring morning when we landed on the runway of a small island airport; yes, picture the television series *Fantasy Island*. I was traveling with a like-minded friend. Six days of intensive instruction to tap into the matrix, the consciousness of the Universe, to communicate with my guide(s). I wanted to see if it was real, if we could connect with our guides and, with proper instruction, have other mystical experiences.

In the best-case scenario, I would have confirmation that death is not what we have been taught, that life continues after death, and that we have nonphysical guides who assist us through each lifetime. Worst-case scenario: I was paying a large amount of money to get away from the stress of work, to have some quiet time on a beautiful island, and to enjoy the benefits of relaxing meditation.

The daily itinerary included waking up to soft, meditative music, breakfast at 8:00 a.m., the first group session around 9:30, and then back to our beds for the first exercise of the day. It felt strange returning to bed at 9:30 every morning. Still, once the headphones were on and the guided meditations began, it was an enjoyable experience… until my sound system glitched. I lay in my room, and there was no sound coming through the headphones—no special meditation that was key in preparing for astral travel. I tried to relax despite feeling confused… *Was this supposed to be a quiet meditation? Maybe I misunderstood the instructions.* After about thirty minutes, I joined the group, which shared some interesting experiences from the first day of exercises. I felt left behind already.

With the new construction of the facility, problems were expected, but I was the only one missing out. *Oh well,* I thought, *it's just the first day. Maybe this is a test for me of letting go of control. Maybe I am supposed to be able to take myself through these relaxation exercises.* The premise was learning to relax the whole body and suspend the thinking process, slowing the brain waves, encouraging me to enter the altered state necessary to allow the awareness of my inner voice, my Higher Self, or any nearby guides. Unfortunately, my frustration and feelings of being behind the progress the group appeared to be making were overwhelming my thoughts and moving me into a lower vibrational frequency instead.

The second day was fraught with more headphone problems. "Come on, Bob!" I would say out loud to the meditation voice—the man's name on the recordings. "No Bob again." I relayed this to the trainer. It was only day two, and while some participants had connected with guides, animal spirit guides, and past loved ones, and some could separate their energy from their physical bodies and experience the benefits of astral travel, I was still fighting to hear Bob through my headphones. Even with the frustration, I found the sessions interesting. I was eventually able to relax and have some of my own compelling adventures while in a deeply relaxed state, but still no guides. Day three was similar; there were only three days remaining to have the experience of my life, to attain a connection to the nonphysical, finally, and with it, the certainty that I craved. But still no Bob. The headphones were silent.

I returned to my room that night; what I needed was chocolate! I rummaged around in my suitcase for a plastic bag of carefully packed, thick chunks of dark chocolate. I found it! But something wasn't right... there were jagged holes torn in the plastic. I looked more closely, and there was one piece of chocolate with several little teeth marks. *Yikes!* A mouse had been dining in my suitcase! For how long? Since I arrived three days earlier? I double-bagged any leftover bite-free pieces and went to the bathroom to throw the chewed chunks in the garbage. When I turned to leave, there were two large piles of mouse poop on the floor. *Of course, that is what happens when you eat your weight in chocolate! Gross!!* It was all gross and funny; maybe the little hungry thief was my guide.

I had some interesting experiences, especially later that week, but I still had doubts. I was working too hard to make things happen, to find proof for myself. Surrendering to metaphysical experiences, or even just meditation, never came naturally to me.

After that trip, I took courses on lucid dreaming, another gateway to meeting our guides. Nothing. I meditated like a trooper, but still nothing. I took a course in Akashic record reading. I could finally settle my mind a little, but still no guide. I practiced with a nearby Kriya Yoga teacher; mantras, chants, meditation, asanas, and I pleaded with Babaji to show himself. Nothing. Was I becoming a spiritual junkie? It was a constant search outside of myself for answers, not just to connect with a guide, but to have access to a loving, nonphysical helper, to wrap me in a warm blanket of approval, of safety, and for someone to tell me I was okay.

I was not even looking for anything special; just *okay* would have sufficed. I continued the search for my guide because without that, who would I receive guidance from? And there were important questions that I sought answers to. There was a part of me that knew it was finally time to open myself up, surrender to connect, and realize that the answers and approval I was looking for would *not* come from *outside* of me. But honestly, I was not there yet.

There was some progress, though, but realizing this at a cognitive level is very different from an inner knowing of how to access and trust. I have learned since, that Active Connection is not likely to happen without an understanding of our energy streams, that we are a part of our particular streams, and that there is only one true source of energy that the streams are a part of, and how *that* is part of me, and I am part of it. (*Just writing that sentence elicited feelings of uncertainty and a desire for more clarity.*)

I could understand that my thoughts lead to whatever my energy feels like. When I sense the energy of others, I can tell if it is kind, peaceful, caring, or attractive to me. I can also tell if it is intense, frustrated, aggressive, indifferent, or uncaring. When I enter a room, I can feel the energy in the room. I can tell if it is a higher frequency or a lower frequency. So, in understanding Active Connection, I would be better able to connect with nonphysical guidance when I am in an energetic space that is more positive, loving, peaceful, etc. That day-to-day plan to be conscious of my energy became my renewed intention, with the ultimate goal of a real connection with my guide(s) through Active Connection.

Vince and Mary's Reflections

We appreciate the explanation of the twelve strands of energy making up the whole. It is easy to understand the concepts of guides and that we are not separate from them. It all helps with understanding "we" consciousness at a different level. Oneness and unity are illustrated quite well in the teaching of the Active Connection.

It is almost a relief to understand that higher vibrations are constantly with us on this journey. Each vibration can help us in a different way. This helps make sense of the term *guides*. Just as important, it helps us understand that we are a part of the energy stream, and there is no separation. It is also helpful to understand the concepts of angels and masters. This takes away even more separation.

Our guides, the higher vibrations of our energy, are always available. In the first several paragraphs that Michele shared with us above, she illustrated how doubt, expectations, and demands keep us from having powerful experiences full of high-level teachings. The beliefs, fears, and anger that we have associated with our religion or spirituality also affect our ability to hear our guides, let alone trust them.

Many have experienced searching for a way to connect. They spend massive amounts of money with very little return. Without addressing our beliefs and learning how to connect with little effort, doubt will create such a low vibration that you will never connect. When we put meaning or expectations on our experiences and results, we drop into a lower vibration. The lower vibration is the true barrier to connection.

We create resistance with our doubts and fears. That resistance can even affect electronic equipment, as Michele experienced in the meditation. The static of low vibration kept her from hearing. Michele suggested in jest that the little mouse was a guide. The possibility is more a probability.

Michele's constant searching with no real success brings up an important thing you must understand. Connection with our guides is vibrational. You must be in a higher vibration. Michele's doubt and expectation were vibrationally low. She was chasing proof from a place of lack. Instead of experiencing the contact she so desperately wanted, she created more lack, doubt, and proof of what she truly believed: There were no guides, or if there were, she didn't *deserve* to connect. There was no trust and surrender. There was no space for the truth to present itself.

Introspective Insights:

(Take a few minutes to journal or meditate on the following questions.)

1. What are your thoughts and feelings about guidance being available to you?
2. Where have you tried to connect to your guides and were affected by beliefs or doubt?
3. How do you support your vibration, and can you use it to connect better?
4. What beliefs and fears might be getting in the way of connecting with your guides?

Receiving Guidance
(AC 12 Jan 24)

We have shared with you this way of connecting to your higher vibrations that is called Active Connection. It is a way for you to receive guidance to support you very clearly on this chosen journey. Although it might be challenging for you at times to trust this guidance and the source of it, know that it is the most effective way for you to receive the support that is constantly available to you.

The Round Table, channeled by Vince Kramer

Many don't believe or trust the process. When I first started getting guidance, I didn't trust the process or even believe that I could tap into guidance. Please share how we receive this guidance.

We seem to be reluctant to notice at times. Active Connection helps us take it further. Can you share more?

> Yes, this is something that most experience for a myriad of reasons.
>
> First, let us share about getting or receiving guidance, and we can explain the resistance at another time. We have shared in the past that you all have access to the vast divine knowledge of the Universe. This goes well beyond any planet, or any level of con-

sciousness experienced in any third-dimensional or fourth-dimensional existence. But each of you is multidimensional and can connect at higher frequencies to different levels of your chosen energy stream.

Each of you is physical *and* nonphysical. The nonphysical part of you has constant contact with these higher-level frequencies you call guides. These guides are constantly assisting you in living your Divine Intent, the reason you chose to come to Earth. It is what many of you refer to as your *why*. The challenge that you are talking about is, first of all, believing that any of you can and actually do receive this information or guidance.

That is very true. Can you share how we receive this guidance?

Let us start with the most resistance-free way that you receive or actually remember this divine knowledge. You are most receptive to receiving and accepting guidance in your sleep. It is a time when you move into the higher vibrations of you without the chaos of the chatter in your head. You are more receptive to the teaching and the learning that it takes to step into your magnificence more fully. During your sleep hours, you can receive information at a level that can't fully be understood during your waking hours until you raise your day-to-day vibration to accept it. You can see this in how quickly you forget your dreams. When you first awaken, you are in the vibration of the message, but then life starts happening and it jars you out the higher vibration.

As you move more toward your day-to-day vibration, you are no longer aligned with the higher vibration of the teaching, and you forget. You personally have experienced many times knowing and understanding something but as soon as you open your eyes, it is gone. Other ways you are given this knowledge or at least nudged toward the information is through messages and promptings. Some of these messages come in the form of what you might call intuition, your inner knowingness. It can be guidance encouraging you to do something or guidance to avoid something.

This thing you call intuition is your connection to the energy of all there is. You also get messages in other ways. It could be a conversation with someone that brings on an aha moment. It might be

> a magazine in a store or a billboard along the street. It could be a conversation you overhear. These are all creations or co-creations of your Higher Self, the nonphysical part of you, getting guidance to you in a way you might pay attention to or notice.

Yes, we seem to be reluctant to notice at times. Active Connection helps us take it further. Can you share more?

> You share many ways for people to tap into this ever-available guidance in your classes. Active Connection has the potential for the clearest way. Connecting to the guides, the higher frequencies are available to you all fluidly and effortlessly if you choose to believe. The answers to all your questions are available if you open yourself to hear, see, and even feel them. As you are given guidance, each of you is different and receives your guidance in your own way. When you use Active Connection, you can document the answers you get and ask your questions in a manner that you do in your everyday life, looking for clarity by asking more pointed questions. As you move fully into the connection with your guides, your vibration increases, just as it does during your sleep. By using Active Connection, you are documenting and can go back and remind yourself what was lost when you moved back into the day.
>
> We will share more later.
>
> For this now, Namaste.

Michele's Musings

So, we all have access to the vast divine knowledge of the Universe, according to this Active Connection (think *The Matrix* movie). Even with that, I continue to struggle despite the efforts I mentioned previously. I also did not understand the concept of multidimensional existence, but I did understand, at some level, that we are both physical and nonphysical, so maybe I did sort of get it.

It sounds like it is the nonphysical part of ourselves, specifically the higher frequencies, that we can connect with and who we call guides, and because the complete spectrum of low to high frequencies is all part of our particular energy streams, we are actually finding our guidance *within* ourselves—not outside of ourselves with some big guide out there. Then we name this higher frequency energy, because that is more palatable for our human brain's understanding. Sounds easy, right? Not for me.

I guess what is less complex for me to understand is that I am responsible for my energetic frequency. I get that. What is the energy I am putting out? Am I connecting with others with loving-kindness? Am I accepting all parts of me in a loving way? Am I judging others and myself less? Am I taking care of myself physically and mentally? Am I generous in my connecting with others but not to the point that I am depleted and not conscious of balancing my time and energy? Most importantly, am I tuning in to the inner voice for guidance, believing it, and trusting it?

These are all works in progress. It is baby steps, keeping it simple, being aware of thoughts and feelings, and using Active Connection once I have increased my energetic vibration. And knowing how to do that and practicing it is taking time. Some days are just crappy! Some people are unkind. Many days I think, *If only I could connect with this higher frequency energy, then the guidance would flow.* The many simple ways to do this are explored in later chapters. My understanding in these earlier days of learning was that guidance from within assists us in living our Divine Intent and our purpose in this life on Earth. It is a common question and one of my big looming questions: Why did I come here? I understood Divine Intent to be our greater purpose in our current lifetime.

The nonphysical energy, as the guides explain through Vince, presents many ways to connect to guidance.

I love sleep. I track my sleep, the hours, the deep sleep, and the REM (rapid eye movement) cycles. My app can confirm whether I had adequate sleep. I joke about that being my means of knowing if I should be tired or not each morning. I started the practice of scribbling the content of my dreams during the night and first thing in the morning when those dreams are most accessible. My research showed that we dream approximately six times per night, so I vowed to capture what I was able to recall. Once awake, I often could not read what I had written, or it made no sense at all, or it was what I later realized to be bits of related occurrences from the previous day regurgitated in fuzzy, dream form.

Hearing the explanation of Trusted Source about what can be gained by being more conscious of the teachings gleaned this way makes it seem worthwhile to commit to further attempts. The first step, though, according to the guides, is to believe that anyone can do it. There are many beliefs I have held (and continue to hold) that limit my ability to achieve this. *What if I interpret the dream messages wrong? What if I did not resonate with the message in the dream or if it did not make sense to me? What other ways might I connect?*

These other ways of connecting include intuition, conversations, books, or movies people suggest, gut feelings, and what I call "shiveries" (hair standing up on my neck or arms). When I wrote my first book, I woke up during the night with inspiration and promptings compelling me to write. Then, I spent years not feeling that. My mojo was gone. And had that been me connecting? Was that what Trusted Source and Vince were trying to get me to connect with? The guidance mentions the higher frequency when we are asleep. Maybe resistance was low during the night, so I was more open to receiving. I enjoyed that happening and missed it when I was trying to write again.

This collaboration with Vince and Mary has awakened it, I am excited to say. I am sleeping less and writing late at night, probably because my resistance is low at that time, and the inspiration and words flow more easily. I feel the ideas (the intuition) pop into my mind like a hot-air popcorn popper. I write them down, and eventually, I sleep.

Ironically, I left my charger for my smart watch back in Canada while I was vacationing in Cancun, Mexico, this past winter. I had come to rely on it, and suddenly, I had no idea what my sleep quality was, and I was still okay. I also did not know my hourly blood glucose, heart rate variance, heart rate, blood pressure, blood oxygen, or steps. And nothing bad happened. Perhaps being less hypervigilant with these things, as well as my micro- and macro-nutrients and net carbs each day, created some space for creativity. Noted.

The third type of connection is Active Connection. I have made valiant attempts through Vince and Mary's teachings. Again, I was like the little engine that could, but *I could not*. The New Age communities I traveled through over the years would say I had way too much gunk, past-life blockages, lineages of bad juju, and generations of trauma, and it was all keeping me from connecting. With mere hundreds or thousands of dollars, I could pay someone to remove the extra... whatever, and there were many things wrong with me! For example, I was never enough, never clear enough, never grounded enough, never clean enough. There seemed to be no digging out of the hole without an abundance of cash. Ironically, another belief system like the one I grew up with is a never-ending to-do list of fixing and listing failures at self-improvement. I have yet to become aware of the cornucopia of existing limiting beliefs acquired through religion, parents, school, society, and media, but it was a start in a new direction of self-awareness and higher vibration, rather than self-loathing and harsh judgment.

Fingers crossed and eyes to the heavens, there will come a day in the not-too-distant future when I will believe in and feel a real-life constant connection to the nonphysical energies in my energy streams. I will use these ways of connecting to increase my energetic frequency, which will further provide answers and guidance. I look forward to living each day in this third dimension we call Earth, maneuvering in a frequency of kindness and love toward myself and others, of seeing the bigger picture of why we are here. But I digress; I may no longer believe in my gunky-ness, but I am very aware that deep in my bones, significant obstacles exist for me, and until these are resolved, I will not experience the feeling of magnificence the guides speak of.

Vince and Mary's Reflections

It is important for us to understand the concepts of multidimensionality, specifically the physical and nonphysical parts of us. Understanding that there is a high vibrational part within that has not been forgotten helps us make sense of our ability to tap into this inner guidance; it becomes clearer to us. Knowing there is this level of connection, we can allow ourselves to get guidance from that all-knowing part.

Guidance is and has always been available throughout our lives. The early part of this session is a good reminder of how we are getting this guidance on a regular basis. The explanation of receiving higher vibrational information and concepts in our sleep makes so much sense. It is also helpful to know why we can't remember the information as we wake up.

We tend not to notice our messages and promptings. There are many reasons for this. However, the reminder that we do and the desire to consciously look for them can change our lives. It is important to pay attention and take action.

Active Connection is what all these chapters are based on. The guidance in this session assures us that we all can connect and be given valuable information in this way. It is a choice and a skill to develop over time if you choose to engage and practice these connections.

Michele points out that we can get our guidance from the higher vibrations we hold. As we coherently align, information can flow more freely. This comes from trust and willingness to allow the information to come through. This alignment comes from choosing to reach and hold a higher vibration. (We will talk about that concept later in the book.)

Once again, Michele shares that her fears are what keep her from connecting in the most effective way. Most of these fears are about being wrong or doing it wrong. We are sure many of you feel the same way, while others have reasons that are fueled by different beliefs. Whatever the reason, know that these beliefs aren't real, and you can choose ones that will support you in getting your guidance.

As Michele honestly discusses her fears, doubts, and resistance in this book, our hope is that you see your own fears, doubts, and resistance. And then like Michele, we hope you will choose to move forward beyond them, to connect with your higher vibrations, and to act on your guidance.

Introspective Insights:
(Take a few minutes to journal or meditate on the following questions.)

1. What would life be like if you could consistently connect with the all-knowing part of you?
2. When did you have an intuitive hit or understanding that left the hairs on your arms standing up?
3. Where have you denied or ignored a message or a prompting out of doubt?
4. What questions would you ask if you could get all the answers through Active Connection?

Obstacles
(AC 5 Jan 24)

> *You are a powerful creator beyond what you can fathom. You create with your thoughts and feelings. The reality you experience is your choice, your creation. This means you have total responsibility for your life. This also means you are not only responsible for your creations, but you are also responsible for the resistance that limits your creations.*
>
> *The Round Table, channeled by Vince Kramer*

Can you share with me what can get in the way of using Active Connection?

> Yes, we would love to help you see the importance of what you are doing. You all have access to the knowledge of the Universe or the knowingness of Source Energy. This includes every thought that has ever been thought and every idea that has ever been had. They are available to you energetically. The obstacles that are in the way of you accessing this information are all internal.
>
> The first obstacle for most is believing you *don't know how* to access this information to get your guidance. The second obstacle is believing whether the information is truly coming *through* to you

or if you are making it up. The third obstacle is remembering or understanding it once you receive it. There are many ways to tap into guidance, and you have found one through Active Connection that helps you and can help many navigate these three main obstacles.

Can you share how Active Connection helps navigate these three obstacles?

First, let us share more about the process; in using the process of your Active Connection, you are actually shifting between the conscious mind and unfiltered receptivity. It is helping your brain see that there is a shift between you choosing the questions and noticing the answers coming in from your connection to all of that. This, over time, trains your brain to let the information come through instead of providing it; the higher you raise your vibration in preparation for your sessions, the more information can come through and with more clarity.

Once again, because you are also energy, this information is available to you all the time. It is a matter of aligning with it and asking for it. Learning how to align your energy is the first step in moving beyond the first obstacle. Then, as we said earlier, there are many ways to tap into this information and guidance. Finding your own individual ways is important. We know you understand this and can help others find their way. Active Connection is a very effective way for most people to get the guidance available.

The second obstacle can be a little more difficult to navigate. Trusting can be difficult, but because you all *know* the information energetically (you have just forgotten) guidance is helping you remember it. As you become more familiar and comfortable with Active Connection, you will notice the answers to your questions get more detailed. You will notice that the answers are things that you would have never said, or at least would have never said in the way that you have written down. You will begin to see this and more if you follow your guidance. You will see real changes in your life. You will start to trust the information that is coming to you, and you will know you are not making it up.

Active Connection is very powerful when it comes to the third obstacle. If you move yourself into the higher vibrations for your Active Connection, as we shared earlier, the information you receive will be at a higher vibration. When you complete your session and move back into your daily vibration, you will forget or maybe not fully understand the guidance you receive.

By following the concepts of Active Connection, you will have written documentation of the guidance that you can go back and reference later. It makes Active Connection unique in the way that those on your Earth can fully tap into the knowledge and guidance available from their higher selves, including the more nonphysical part of themselves and higher vibrational guidance.

We want to remind all as we close, it is important that each of you fully connect with the guidance available.

In this now, Namaste.

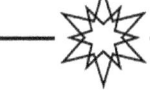

Michele's Musings

It has not been an easy process. Recognizing and then overcoming the obstacles in fully connecting has been gradual for me. The first obstacle, knowing how to connect, has taken much practice and I admit that I have been hot and cold with this over time. Belonging to a community that teaches, coaches, and supports in this endeavor has helped for accountability and in integrating a more consistent practice. It has been like strengthening a muscle. There is no *one and done*. Vince and Mary's programs have helped me to understand the importance and necessity of raising my vibration in the process of aligning and then accessing nonphysical guidance. But, learning how is not the complete picture.

The second obstacle, trust, was a doozy! For someone who tends to be skeptical, my default—when I tuned into higher frequency energy—was to question whether I was actually connecting. How interesting that I could trust the connection if I paid *someone else* to do it but had little confidence in my own direct access. With time and practice I experienced feeling connected in my writing and especially tuning in via Active Connection. At times, I would revert back to disempowering beliefs, i.e., that this was for more gifted people, and how embarrassing to think I might be imagining it, or worse, faking it. I know now that I have been suspicious of and judged that in others.

For the second obstacle, initially I did not believe it was real, even when I just wrote as ideas popped into my head. The effort was there, but not the results. Incidentally, all those thoughts and feelings were the lower vibration of doubt, the kind that gets in the way of accessing answers, guidance, and information.

When I was completing Active Connection exercises during the Take a Quantum Leap program with Vince and Mary in 2023, I was committed to finishing all of them; I had notebooks full of writing. I spent less time with thoughts that I was making it up and more time believing I was really connecting.

In the early days, I had this thing about getting everything done before I sat down to do my practice, whatever that may have been in any given month. The dishes done, laundry done, or at least a load in the washer, sending a response text to a loved one or two, checking my email, tidying up, and having everything in its place before sitting and potentially settling my mind. *If I was truly progressing on a path of evolving or expanding, should I not have been able to sit anytime, anywhere, and tune in?* It always had to be the last thing left to do, which did seem strange: Was meditation not a priority? Did I just require no clutter in my environment to be in a space of relaxation? The problem with this issue is the lists were never done most days, so I waited until my guided nighttime meditation just before drifting off, rather than focusing with intention, energy, and purpose.

I had taken numerous courses, including meditation, some purchased courses more helpful than others, and intuitive sessions of all kinds. I was likely excessive, and more often than not, foolish in what I would refer to as "research for my next book." I was secretly hoping the next shiny thing or person would point me toward a "proper" way to tune in and ultimately discover my true nature. I understand everyone needs to make money and the exchange-of-services concept, and I contributed with curiosity to the financial support of numerous New Age influencers, and yet, I was left with more doubt, more questions than answers. I am grateful for these significant teachers. I paid to learn the valuable lesson of what was *not* resonating, with many of the experiences achieving the same feeling of old belief systems. Had I replaced the dogmatic tenets of religion with the never good enough and never doing enough of various New Age ideologies? And I was still searching *outside* of myself in trusting connection.

Then came Human Design, a system that marries ancient wisdom with science. I was intrigued by this relatively new personality testing/energy system. My chart drew me in instantly. I needed to know my Type and all the rest! I spent the first year of retirement with that focus and enjoyed working with people and their charts. This system was a satisfying mix and a balance of old and new that felt distanced from full-on woo-woo, but it was not the connection with nonphysical energy that satisfied my need for answers to the big questions.

While exploring metaphysics and healing modalities, I did not simply read about each; I was determined to experience every system I became aware of. The mediumship course was intriguing and costly, and I enjoyed some interesting experiences. Was it really my dad that I felt communicating with me? I like to think so. Was his energy connecting with my thoughts and with my heart? The channeling course also promised the potential to connect with the nonphysical. Some gems surfaced, but not the connection or certainty I was seeking on an experiential level.

With more recent learnings, especially with the Take a Quantum Leap program over the past year, I have gained some understanding about connecting. I finally (and gratefully) experienced guidance, but obstacles remained. I had a cognitive understanding of *how* to connect; I had learned that guidance or the connection with my guides was coming from my personal energy stream, the higher frequency part of my energy along this spectrum of energies. I also learned that without practice, the higher-frequency information I was seeking would not be accessible. I would continue to question its validity and would not remember or understand it because I did not consistently believe it was real. How could I change that belief, adapt to connecting in a way that suited me, *and* commit to practicing raising my frequency daily, especially before trying to connect?

I purchased a session with Vince and The Round Table, and during the session, I was excited to learn through higher frequency energies that my energy streams are the colors orange, pink, and turquoise. After researching the Archangels associated with each of the colors, I could name the energies that I was trying to connect with as Uriel, Chamuel (or Ariel), and Haniel. Still, without really feeling like I knew they were *there* or *here* as a part of my energy, it felt like talking to a wall or just throwing questions out there and hoping some answers would surface. The second obstacle, which was related to believing it was all real, needed further exploration of my beliefs about who we are, why we are here, and about guidance being accessible to everyone. I was aware that transforming my beliefs and expanding my perception would only happen with practice, with raising my energetic frequency daily and connecting from that space.

It felt like a good start. My family would say that I normally enjoy telling certain people what to do, but in this instance, I would gently invite readers to consider the old saying, "What do we have to lose?" Well, just imagine, what do we have to *gain* by recognizing and removing the obstacles to connecting with nonphysical, high vibration energy? It could include the deep transformation available when we choose to trust and open to our truest selves, the limitless possibilities, the releasing of the old paradigm, and expanding our awareness by trusting and accepting we are all Universal Energy. With that, we are the beneficiaries, the rightful owners and recipients of constant connection to unlimited knowledge and guidance.

Vince and Mary's Reflections

The three obstacles that get in our way of tapping into this knowledge and help available come from those around us. At least initially, the beliefs and doubts of others become our doubts and fears. The judgments of those we trust have left us believing there is something wrong with us if we believe we have a connection. The guidance in this session attempts to set us free.

The guidance shared in this session provides a very understandable explanation and solid case for us all to use Active Connection to connect with and receive counsel from the highest vibrational part of ourselves and the energy streams we chose to represent. It requires us to be willing to accept and trust that we all have the capability. We know from experience how effective Active Connection is, and we encourage you to learn how to use it to connect with the divine knowledge available to us all.

Michele bravely admits to what most of us experience when it comes to trying and trusting Active Connection. As the guides shared, the three obstacles keep us from tapping into our guidance, and Michele illustrates how that might look. In sharing the need to get everything done before she attempted her Active Connection, she shows us how the resistance looks. It might be different for all of us, but you can see through Michele's eyes how it showed up for her.

Michele's honesty and vulnerability can support you in your endeavors to connect to your guides. She helps you see that it is a journey of trust and acceptance. At the same time, she shares that it takes a willingness to believe in the connection that we all have.

> **Introspective Insights:**
> (Take a few minutes to journal or meditate on the following questions.)
> 1. What are your beliefs around being able and knowing how to tap into guidance?
> 2. Where are you challenged with believing and trusting the guidance you receive?
> 3. How can you remember the information you receive, and how could retaining the information benefit you?
> 4. What would your life look like if you were able to receive guidance you could trust on demand?

Purpose
(AC 9 Jan 24)

There are no mistakes or coincidences in the Universe. You chose to incarnate on the Earth for many multidimensional reasons. The choice in the third dimension was to fully live a life in a way that you use your gifts and talents in alignment with who you are and why you chose to be. This is your Unique Purpose.

The Round Table, channeled by Vince Kramer

Would you take some time to share about earthly purpose? We are all in search of purpose. Help us understand.

> Yes, we will be happy to share this important idea with all of you. We have shared the concept of multidimensionality with you many times, and this is yet another opportunity to look at it and understand that you are multidimensional and are living multidimensionally.
>
> To give you the most pertinent information in our session together, we want to share purpose in two broad categories: universal purpose and earthly purpose.

That would be helpful. Can you explain the universal purpose first?

Yes, we will, especially because universal purpose includes your purpose on Earth. As you know and share in your work, there is one energy, and you all are that energy, each representing a stream or a combination of streams. Universal or source energy is constantly expanding, and that expansion happens in the third and fourth dimensions.

Each of you is a stream or a combination supporting this expansion by coming to a 3D planet to cause it. You cause the expansion through the experience of the low and high vibrations of your stream or streams and then expanding it into yet a higher vibration.

This expansion is supported at all frequencies of the streams of energy you represent. In simple terms, you are on the planet Earth to experience the highs and lows of who you are and expand beyond the highs. In doing this, you are a participant in expanding the Universal Energy that you aren't just a part of—*you are*.

When we hear that source or God energy wants to experience itself, is this what it means?

Yes, that is exactly what it means. Now let us share with you the concept of earthly purpose. First, know that as energy, you can say you choose this existence to support the expansion. Before you were ever born, you chose the planet where you were going to live, this existence, and the difference you were going to make. Knowing that each stream of energy—in this case, each individual person making their difference on the planet—would help others make their difference, and the result of all making their respective differences would result in this universal expansion that we explained earlier.

In choosing this difference, let's say the wheels of energetic support started to turn. You chose your parents and where you would live and made what you might refer to as soul agreements, all to provide you the opportunity and circumstances to create and co-create a life. And every part of that life was to prepare you for and then to fully live this life you are meant to live, to make the difference you chose to make.

As each of you makes your difference, others have an opportunity to make theirs. It is like a puzzle: When you fit in your piece of the puzzle, others may see where theirs fits.

This is the magic of the ebb and flow of the Universal Energy. Each part, the energy streams, and the combinations make up the whole and *are* the whole at the same time. There is more for you to know about purpose, as in, what it all means and what part each purpose plays in the overall purpose of universal expansion. We will share that at another time, but at this *now,* know that each of you plays an integral part in helping each other in the experience of making that difference you chose to make in this world you also chose.

In this now, Namaste.

Michele's Musings

During my initial session with Vince and The Round Table, I was still testing the waters. Was Vince's channeling the real deal? I had seen several people do what seemed magical; a few were good enough to challenge my skepticism. Could they really connect with the matrix, with Universal Energy and all the knowledge within, or with beings or energy that could not be seen or heard by most humans? I was looking for certainty because that would mean opening a Pandora's box of beliefs that would no longer be true. I had heard the concept of multidimensionality but had yet to understand it. *How many dimensions are there? Is it common knowledge that we exist physically in 3D, the third dimension, and are all the higher dimensions invisible to us because they are in the nonphysical?*

Sitting on Zoom with Vince and my higher frequency energies, a.k.a. The Round Table, these guides—as parts of me and my energy streams—were explaining to my physical, 3D self the concept of multidimensions and that we chose, while we were not physical yet (before we were born) where we would live and who our parents would be. That seemed like a leap! Then I remembered my youngest son at an early age, frustrated with us, saying, "Nice parents I picked!" Then, another day came to mind when he was very young. We were driving in the city where we lived when he pointed to a street and said, "That's where I lived when I was big." Do we choose our parents? Did we exist in other lifetimes? I had experienced some convincing intuitive people, some who called themselves "evidential mediums," and there were a few convincing channels. One that stood out in my early days of exploring was Esther Hicks connecting with the nonphysical energies she called Abraham.

My scope of focus on the expenditure of time and money had narrowed to the very few that I had resonated with. I like to call them "high frequency energy connectors." Unfortunately, the word *channel* has had a negative connotation over the years, even though the term appropriately describes what was occurring: being a channel for energy or information. Shirley MacLaine and her notoriety for her nonmainstream spirituality and beliefs of reincarnation came to mind.

Rather than continuing the wide and shallow exploration, I was drawn to expand my curiosities into a more narrow and deep perception through working with Vince and Mary. Vince's story outlined in their book was convincing, but experiencing The Round Table's connection through Vince, my participation in Vince and Mary's courses, and my connection with them dissolved much doubt. With this significant progress in my own expanded perception of life and the world, one would think that I would have, by this time, been able to believe in my own connections and trust the guidance. Yes, I had begun to be more open to trusting, but surrendering was still hot and cold.

It is definitely easier to believe only what our five senses show us. Despite my efforts, I had never experienced seeing deceased people or angels or even hearing one little peep from nonphysical energy.

What I *had* experienced, even though I was not well-versed in quantum physics, was the energy part of myself and others, how people's energy introduces them before they say a word, how we enjoy some people's company and not others: It is our energetic frequency. I knew we had a spider sense or gut feelings, but we never referred to that as energy. I have also been aware that higher frequency energy in people is sensed as enjoyable, loving, kind, authentic, fun, and pleasant, and lower frequency energy as sad, judgmental, angry, intense, stressed, depressed, vindictive, phony, or just generally negative. The guide's message in the Active Connection explains Earth's purpose as higher frequency, and even though as physical beings we experience the full spectrum of low and high throughout our days, the sweet spot is achieving high frequency and beyond.

So, my career in corrections and addictions was not my only purpose or my primary purpose, really. It was to experience what happens as my energy expands in a way that I can see myself and others from that expanded perspective. What would happen if we connected with and supported each other as we all discovered life's bigger questions while experiencing higher-frequency energies?

The Round Table invited a new perspective during my initial session, startling me onto an exciting trajectory of deepening and expanding into new ways of experiencing my true self, accepting the belief that I was not done, I was not too old, and my beliefs about retirement were just beliefs. I had believed my age meant I no longer had anything to offer and that in my late fifties (at the time of that first session), any contribution would be worthless or just plain foolish. But what if my work experience and life experiences were (as with everyone) valuable and could be well-received by and helpful to others? I was unsure where the belief about aging originated, and I realized then that changing it could present interesting opportunities in my "old age." But now what?

More work to do? Yes, and probably the most important and real work to this point.

When I chose to take Vince and Mary's program Take a Quantum Leap, I was skeptical. It was a significant investment, but I was committed to participating fully to see what it had to offer. I was determined to get my money's worth. And there was something different about how I had resonated with that initial session with The Round Table.

The course proved to be challenging. One might question why someone would choose to dive into their psyche and their innermost self to question everything, especially previously held beliefs, but I knew there was more. I was determined to experience it. I felt the floor drop out from under me a few times, ironically just prior to extraordinary rewards. I was finally able to find answers to my existential questions. But a voice surfaced from time to time. Was I being duped again? It had happened in a significant way before, through the fear and shame-based religious beliefs I grew up with. Of course, this was not the same; I was older, a critical thinker, and just doing research. (That is what I had told myself to justify the investment before every course and intuitive session.) Ultimately, my motivation was to learn how to master my mind and learn how to react less or not at all. If I was here to accomplish some sort of mission, what was it? I wanted the skills to transform a crappy day into a less crappy day, to change my perception from victimhood to empowerment, and most importantly, to enjoy a default emotional state of high frequency and ideally, keep that state as my default.

Looking back, I see the course was early in the excavation process, opening me to see myself, others, and the world differently, more deeply, more realistically, in the bigger picture sense, and mastering my mind, as they say. What would my day-to-day life and relationships look like if I responded more, reacted less, suffered less, and felt more joy? What if I knew who I truly was, why I was here, and my purpose in an earthly sense as well as in a universal sense?

One of the most significant things I was hoping to gain was being able to maneuver in a more conscious way, but as fun as that sounds, I had yet to understand what that really meant.

This session with The Round Table was where I learned my particular energy streams: orange, turquoise, and pink, associated with Archangels Uriel, Haniel, and Chamuel, respectively. None of the big guns! I thought twice about any complaints, though, as I had three guides! And I needed them all! And really, would the Archangels not all be considered *big guns* in the angelic realm hierarchy? And is there a hierarchy? Angels, it was explained, are not associated with a religious concept. They are energies that are within every person's energy streams along with their own energy, all connected to source energy, God/Goddess energy, or Universal Energy, whatever our human brains feel comfortable calling it. Looking back, in my visits to the convent, I had perceived the angels in a similar arena of beliefs as I did the judge-y, old, bearded man in the sky, as well as a few other nuggets, including hell and original sin.

I took a bit of a plunge and considered embracing angels in this new context as guides, helpers, and part of me, or, more accurately, part of my energetic field. Their higher frequency would be where I could access guidance, information, and support. I felt excitement having the three Archangels to myself, or sort of to myself. I researched these lesser known of the angelic realm and found some interesting and relatable tidbits, including that they were two males and one female... even though they are not really gendered. Not only had I reopened the door, albeit slightly, to the angels, but also these energies, including my own energy, would potentially be assisting me in finally learning my purpose and why I was here on Earth.

I learned my earthly purpose or Divine Intent (more about that reference later) during the Take a Quantum Leap program. Initially, I became aware of my "quintessence" (defined in the course as the real and concentrated essence of me, the energy I put out into the world), then acknowledged my gifts and talents (what I had learned and developed to this point), and learned to use those to live my purpose, to empower others. As I understood the guides in this Active Connection, my earthly purpose is part of the universal purpose, connecting with others, assisting and supporting others, loving-kindness and service to others, all in the pursuit of expanding our energy and the ultimate intent of being part of this ever-expanding Universal Energy. What were the ways that I could make a difference in the lives of others? Then, how could those things make a difference to the expansion of the Universe's energy, no matter how seemingly insignificant? Imagine no longer seeing ourselves as separate but as *all connected* to each other and to the prime source of Universal Energy, which is the source of all our energy streams.

In my travels, I had heard of *enlightenment*, which sounded daunting, and *ascension*, which sounded unattainable. Plus, ascending and leaving behind loved ones felt unbearable, but *expansion* sounded positive, inclusive, and loving. I resonated with that.

Vince and Mary's Reflections

Have you ever considered yourself multidimensional? If you have, what about your purpose being multidimensional? What a concept—definitely a new paradigm. There are deep and important reasons we chose to come to Earth. We are here to expand Universal Energy. It is a concept beyond question when you consider what is shared in this guidance. A daunting task to the human mind, it is explained so well in this session that it is easy to accept.

At first, the statement "You are here to experience the highs and lows of who you are" is hard to digest. But when you consider what was said, it helps make sense of our lives and the highs and lows. It illustrates a purpose for everything we experience. There truly are no mistakes or coincidences, and everything does happen for a reason. We are all here to live and place our puzzle pieces so others can find where they belong.

In sharing her skepticism and experiences with her son, Michele helps us see how answers and proof are available if we are willing to look and listen. When we are willing to start asking the questions, the answers become available. In sharing her continued vulnerability, we hope you not only see yourself in her doubt but also that you aren't alone in any of those feelings you might have. Her learning to trust opens possibilities for you.

So many beliefs we have carried from childhood or developed along the way have disempowered us. In believing she had nothing left to offer, Michele almost stopped living on purpose, stopped making the difference only she could make. She is not alone. This is very prevalent, especially in Western society. Let her new understanding motivate you to discover and fully live your purpose. Use her new understanding and experiences to help you remove your doubt and choose to pursue all you are meant to be.

Introspective Insights:
(Take a few minutes to journal or meditate on the following questions.)

1. What are your feelings on having two big reasons to be on the Earth at this time?
2. Where have you doubted your usefulness or reason for being alive?
3. When has doubt, fear, or belief stopped you from seeing your importance and reason for being on Earth at this time?
4. How would you like to make a difference, and what part would that play in universal expansion?

Resistance
(AC 6 Dec 23)

There is much resistance to even believing the possibilities that are in front of you, as well as your ability to accomplish what you can imagine. Know that everything you dream can be yours. Everything you desire can be yours if you choose your wants and desires based on fully living your reason for being.

The Round Table, channeled by Vince Kramer

Talk to me about our resistance to fully being who we are meant to be and following the guidance that we ask for to get there. Can you explain?

> It all seems so perplexing, doesn't it? You, the human race, and all 3D realms don't want to be conscious of your lives because of the beliefs that you are or have been wrong. It is complex for the development level of your brain in the context you hold in your mind. It is made complex because of the refusal to accept that it is all truly on the inside. There are many reasons not to accept. All these reasons are generated from how you are designed to live and perceive in your world and in your bodies. Your perception of

your very existence physically is all based on your five senses. These senses are what you all believe.

The physical world around you is the true third dimension, but the interpretation is that you are separate from all the things you are perceiving through your senses. This alone allows you to hold on to the belief that you can't change what you believe the problem is.

What is on the outside? The other concept we want you to consider is around the fact that you are in control of your reality and the fear that if you are, you can't create what you want or, more debilitating, you created what you have up till now. There is also the human tendency to take the easy road, the path of least effort. You even share in your programs the phrase "the path of least action" or "the least-action pathway."

Basically, humans have evolved into unchecked acceptance, accepting whatever comes their way, believing it isn't ever going to get any better because they have no real control. This leads to accepting what is in their perception and believing it is good enough. Another human mind trick is *not* to try, so there is no chance of failure, but the only true failure is the failure to try, the failure to start, or, as you have termed on your planet, "the failure to thrive."

You all must choose to be who you are meant to be, choose to start, and choose to follow the guidance you are. You all seem so sure that guidance can only come from outside of you, but the guidance comes *from* you, the highest frequencies *of* you.

For you are source energy, and source energy is you.

In this now, Namaste.

Michele's Musings

My confession, of course, is that I was resistant to this one! I bristled at the question initially *of being fully who we are meant to be,* as it felt like a *should* or requirement coming from outside of me. What if the wording was "who we came here to be" or "who we chose to come here to be." *Who we are meant to be* felt like someone was requiring me to be who *they* meant for me to be, and I had heard that song before. No thank you. Was I just misunderstanding the phrase? Or should I consider it was really *me* making plans for *myself* in this life?

Even perceiving it this way, I felt some resistance to the concept. What would others think if I changed significantly? How difficult would it be to move forward, to take the plunge, and what would that look like, living a fully purposeful life? To be honest, I felt like I had not yet experienced the *living fully* part. I learned how to listen to guidance during Take a Quantum Leap, and there were times when I felt strongly that I was receiving guidance through Active Connection exercises. Still, my belief in the guidance was inconsistent, and eventually, thoughts of doubt would overpower any confidence I may have gained. How could I follow the guidance that I had a flimsy belief in? And how could it help me if I was not trusting it fully? Considering the work I had done to date, maybe the resistance to move forward and to trust the guidance had something to do with conditioning; guidance is for gurus, priests, shamans, and pastors, not for just anybody.

For decades, I lived by a list of rules. Be a good girl. Never be wrong. Please others at any cost. Take care of others before myself. *Do not* express anger or show emotions other than cheery ones. These rules were put in place in my formative years, then compounded and reinforced for protection by my subpersonalities, the ever-critical judgmental voice we have in our heads. Follow the rules, and don't rock the boat! Don't speak up! Don't upset other people! I fell in line nicely, mostly to avoid being rejected, and I am aware of how dramatic this may sound but doing so felt necessary for survival. I needed to feel safe, but often didn't. The unsafe feeling was deeply ingrained at a young age and grew more powerful as I grew.

My subpersonalities, throughout this time, floated near the surface, cresting when necessary, leading me safely away from the storms and remaining a loyal part of me. On one hand, I was falling in line and avoiding rejection; on the other, these were the rules that were reinforced at home and at my religious school (the two schools in my small prairie town were referred to as the public school and the separate school, which I attended). Also, the message of the church I attended contributed to irrational guilt, a broad swath of internalized shame (no corner of my psyche was left untouched), never feeling good enough, believing others' thoughts and feelings were more important than mine, believing something was wrong with me, and feeling different from other people because of all of this. And who decided that endless self-improvement was virtuous?

There is nothing wrong with self-improvement in and of itself. Still, it is low frequency energy when we internalize societal pressure, including social media pressure, to always be better. All of this to please others to avoid rejection, and more recently, for younger generations of poor souls, compounded by an insatiable need for likes and followers.

The most significant belief and challenge related to this Active Connection has been my struggle to accept that guidance comes from inside, not outside, where, ironically, my valiant efforts have resided. I understand that most of us believe only what we see, feel, taste, hear, smell, and touch, so our experiences are limited to these five senses, which leaves less room for perceived uncertainty.

I could also relate to *not wanting* to be conscious due to the beliefs around being wrong. As mentioned earlier, beliefs about me, others, and the world were infused from early years, and later, every bit of knowledge was sought from mostly New Age teachers and gurus of all stripes. The belief that guidance comes from others was sewn into the fabric of my psyche. I was wrong for so many years! And what if I am wrong again? Tell me who I am, please! Tell me if I am good enough! Am I good enough yet? And please tell me that I am special!

Shifting away from dependence on outside acceptance and accessing pertinent information about myself was not yet an inside job. I was managing the wolf at the door, my ultimate motivators were to answer to my subpersonalities, please others, and avoid rejection.

Another downside to this outer focus for answers, guidance, and approval was consistent with my career responsibilities. When I was introduced to a new way of treating addictions, it was like hearing the good news! We were not diseased from birth, *WOW*! Seeing that we could assist others in empowering themselves to change their behavior and that this was not a lifetime infliction on us when we were powerless babies was such a relief! The perspective was grounded in research, years of studies related to behavioral change, and lived experiences of people struggling, and it included a less deterministic way of treating problematic behavior. We likely all know of a person who continues down the road of addiction while the next person seems to have pivoted and succeeded with very few setbacks if any at all.

Many are more prone due to environmental, social, biological, or psychological influences, but everyone is capable of choosing differently. At the center where I worked, I witnessed clients' relief when they internalized that they *could* change and that it was *up to them* to create a different life. Many had felt powerless to that point, either through the conditioning of apathy and victimhood, believing they had "bad genes," blaming their upbringing, or from low frequency messages of hopelessness and helplessness, and many others suffered from unresolved (and often unknown) trauma.

The underlying philosophy was not about fixing or changing people but of helping them empower themselves and affirming that they had control over their lives. Although it is easier for some than others, we *can* choose differently. It is a liberating concept: We are not victims of circumstances, only of perceptions. Could we create what we want? Anything? It required challenging long-held beliefs and self-fulfilling prophecies. We often heard, "My mom was an alcoholic, I can't help it," or "It's in my genes," etc.

I remember hundreds of clients discussing the worst addiction—smoking; so why did we not call them diseased from birth and for life? Nicotine addiction is really not viewed as genetic the way harmful use of other addictive substances is. There are historical reasons why we have viewed addiction in certain ways over the years. Gratefully, it continues to be a dynamic field of study, and as we learn more, we adjust our views and how we assist people.

The new paradigm comes to mind… at a human-to-human energetic level, how we connect with and help others struggling has evolved into a higher frequency way of assisting and supporting them in acknowledging and remembering their power to choose differently, and, in doing so, they transform their own lives. Many refer to this as *agency* (the sense of control over our lives, our capacity to influence our thoughts and behavior, and confidence in our ability to handle a wide range of situations, *thanks Webster)*.

Another layer to believing we can make things happen in our lives is feeling the responsibility when things fall apart. The good part says, "Hey, look! I can create and co-create!" The not-so-good says, "Oh crap! Look what I created!"

So, do we have agency, or are we pinballs in a machine, rolling wherever the flippers send us? Trusted Source uses the words *unchecked acceptance*, referring to accepting whatever comes our way, taking the easy road. I relate to the accepting part, but is it the easy road? Here is an example that comes to mind: An area that I would very much like to be accepting of and take the easy road is with my body. Let us say that I believe I have no control over the wellness of my body; it is genetic; I cannot help it; it is too hard to do anything differently, etc. I imagined it; I could eat whatever I wanted, whenever I wanted, and sit on the couch, endlessly streaming as much as I wanted. How great would that be, having no worries in the world related to eating and chilling.

That would be fun for a while, especially the eating part. Then the physical ailments would surface, because our bodies cannot support us when we do not support them. Then, we would complain about our ailments, which we have had a part in creating. Then, as the complaining continued, eventually other people would walk the other way when they see us coming. The things we think and do and how we behave toward others results in increasing or decreasing our energetic frequency, which means we have agency; *we are not victims*. I did not have to look far to find the scientific studies on how the body holds anger, negativity, sadness, loneliness, depression, victimhood, judgment, etc., and then notifies us in a myriad of ways: anxiety, illnesses related to stress and other emotions, a painful medical diagnoses, or serious problems within any and all systems of the body, including cancer.

So, in the big scheme of things, is the lazy road the easy road?

And finally, yes, I agree to start being who I came here to be and to follow the guidance leading me to what that is. I choose *not* to be lazy, to continue to learn and grow, and to take responsibility daily for my energy and what I create. The new paradigm is a shift toward living in the highest frequencies, guided by our emotions, increasing our frequency through our thoughts and actions and how we connect with others in a loving, kind, and connected way. On the scale of emotions (it is worth googling), we have the lowest emotions (fear, despair, and powerlessness), the highest emotions of joy, empowerment, and love, and all the emotions in between. The high energetic frequencies equate to knowing, trusting, createing, and co-creating the things we want. When our frequencies are higher, our energy expands. When this aligns with what we came here to do and to be, we are moving away from the old paradigm of feeling separate from each other and expanding into the new paradigm of oneness.

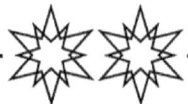

Vince and Mary's Reflections

Once again, it comes down to beliefs. Our resistance to living the life we are meant to live and following our guidance is based on the beliefs that we are separate from everything, that everything happens *to* us, and that we have no control. These beliefs have been passed down from generation to generation. They are beliefs held by society and used by all of us to stay safe by staying the same. In many cases, they are used against us by others to control us.

We aren't separate, and we create our own reality. Until we accept that responsibility and fact, we will live in fear and make ourselves victims of the resistance. We must honor who we are and choose to follow the guidance available to be all we are meant to be. We must refuse to let old, outdated beliefs and fears keep us stuck or afraid.

Michele begins her musing with resistance. It is a very common resistance: "You aren't going to tell me what to do." This still comes from a place of separation—something on the outside telling me what to do. We all put meaning to things based on our beliefs and how we show up. These projections are crippling as they try to make others wrong and give control to others. This type of thinking makes us victims. We have been taught to live from this fear and it keeps us in the low vibration of fight or flight. And then she followed with the second most common reason to stay the same: "What will other people think?" Her honesty is helpful in seeing ourselves in our own fears and beliefs.

In sharing her list of rules, Michele shows how our conditioning and self-chosen perceptions have created much of our resistance. These rules, at best, slow us down and, at worst, stop us from moving at all. Many of the rules are imposed on us, and others are willingly accepted. Either way, they are the resistance keeping us from living the life we are meant to live.

When Michele mentions self-improvement being low frequency, the lower vibration is because of the expectation of being what everyone else is. It is in following someone else's way. It is essential for you to find your way. And the best way to do that is to find help from someone who understands the concept. However, as Michele stated, the subpersonalities are fighting any change at all. They justify all the reasons, and we tend to follow them blindly. We believe those voices in our heads as they strive to keep us the same. We see the difference in Michele's example of changing the narrative and quieting the voices of addiction.

When Michele shares about her body and her health, she illustrates circumstances that we all experience, although not necessarily with our bodies. We have been taught that if we change how we think or talk about something, we will change our behavior. That is true if the thoughts during our conscious and subconscious times are the same. If they are not, they compete. Because we spend most of our time in the subconscious, those beliefs win out. We are in control of our reality, and choosing to remove the resistance by changing our beliefs will set us free.

Introspective Insights:
(Take a few minutes to journal or meditate on the following questions.)

1. What would be different if you chose to see the oneness of the Universe?
2. Where have your beliefs been keeping you stuck?
3. What voices in your head are keeping you from the life you are meant to live?
4. If you allowed yourself to hear and follow the guidance, how might your life be different?

New Paradigm
(AC 19 Jan 24)

There is a new paradigm afoot. Your planet as the macrocosm, just as you as the microcosm, is moving into a new level of consciousness. The movement is from an "I" consciousness, which is based in separateness and duality, into a "we" consciousness based in oneness and unity.

The Round Table, channeled by Vince Kramer

Much has been shared about the new paradigm. Can you spend some time explaining what you mean by it?

> Yes, certainly. This subject might take many sessions with you to explain fully. Let's start with the overall movement in your planet's consciousness. Every planet goes through an evolution. It can be a very extensive conversation. To gain a full understanding, it is best to share the shift that you are experiencing on Earth at this time.

> The collective energy and, therefore, the overall consciousness of your planet have been expanding. This expansion is a movement toward understanding and eventually living from the knowing that you are all one. Accepting, if you will, not just at the mind level but every level, that there is one energy, and you all make up the one

energy. There is only one. Knowing, living, and being all one is basically the new paradigm. Over the coming sessions, we will explain that in more ways.

Vince: Thank you. That would help tremendously. Can you say more about the paradigms, the old and the new?

The paradigm that the Earth's collective is living in this moment is what we have shared in the past as the *I consciousness*. When we say collective, we are referencing the vibration of the combination of all the humans on your planet.

You could say, for simplicity's sake, it is the average. (It is more complex than that, though.) The *I consciousness* (the old paradigm) is based in separation or duality. It can be seen or experienced in I, mine, and in you and yours. The physicality of each of you supports it. Your five senses support that you are separate from each other. Everything is on the outside of you. This paradigm is of "things happen to me" and "either/or." It gives your power away and leaves you operating from the belief that you are living a predetermined life and that you have no control.

There is also a separation in each of you and an internal conflict that keep you stuck. The new paradigm is what we all call the *we consciousness*, the paradigm of oneness. The paradigm of unity. There is no separation. There is no separation in who you are. There is no separation from the inside to the outside. Things happen because of you and for you. What is on the inside is on the outside. What is on the outside is on the inside. This is a shift that has been happening for hundreds of years and will fully happen soon.

In this now, Namaste.

Michele's Musings

Okay, so I have to say this one freaks me out a little or a lot depending on the day. When I was on the New Age train, there was much talk about "the big shift" or "the ascension." I believe it was a story told through the ages, originating in biblical times, to terrorize people so they would fall in line. Try to sleep at night after perusing the Book of Revelation. That was the very early days of FOMO (fear of missing out). The chosen few would ascend, leaving loved ones behind on this crappy Earth. Who would want to miss that bus? And there is another timeline to be cognizant of. You must hurry, fix yourself, and be worthy to be chosen. Drum roll... it is said to be happening in 2027, a mere three years away as I write this.

While reading this Active Connection and observing my reaction, or my overreaction, I found it interesting that the guide's response did not describe mass chaos, Earth annihilation, and other disaster stories that went through my mind.

My disaster stories started when I was a little girl. I could barely reach the windows in the farmhouse where I grew up. As soon as I heard the first sounds of thunder, I would run for the mason jar of holy water, dip my little pointer finger in, and outline a cross on each window. I was terrified of lightning striking the house; I felt this was the only way to keep me and my family safe!

This irrational fear continues today. I must avoid being blindsided! If I prepare myself for all possibilities, I feel safer somehow. (As I said, it's irrational.) When we were ice fishing on the frozen lake, I was certain that our large, heavy truck would go under. After arriving at the edge of the frozen lake, my husband stopped the truck and told me to take off my seatbelt. I loudly said, "No way!!!" He explained that if we went through the ice, we could get out of the truck quicker. I did not have my watch on then to check my heart rate. I did not need to!

Added to the adventures that day, a large wolf was visible every few minutes through a wall of snow and fog, each time lurking closer to our fabric ice shack. We survived that day. I am Henny Penny in the *Chicken Little* children's book. "The sky is falling!" My eyes are forever to the skies in the summer, expecting tornadic activity to be imminent in my area of the country. Traveling to Vancouver Island, I imagined The Big One, the earthquake that would bury the West Coast upon my arrival. It did not. And do not get me started on how I prepare myself to fly 37,000 feet in the air. Thankfully, I have gotten less anxious—so far, without medication—but there were years that I played a clever mind game; I would take a real chocolate bar in my purse, not bitter dark chocolate because if we were going down, I would be eating the real deal, guilt-free. Again, irrational. Logically, I knew if we were going down, the last thing on my mind would be the chocolate bar!

There are many reasons for my worst-case scenario default position and lack of an internal sense of safety. Throughout my life, I perceived dangers lurking around every corner. It was a stream of low-grade anxiety. Past experiences solidified the belief that the world is scary and hostile. I learned we are all separate and competing; we must fight because our world is about survival of the fittest; and as an internal conflict example, relationships with other people are transactional or conditional. If I said no to people, I would be rejected. I believed I had to act a certain way to be accepted and loved. The reasons behind these disempowering beliefs and the adaptive, protective mechanisms (my ego or subpersonalities) are complex, difficult, and painful. Despite that, or because of it, I am here. I am okay. More than that: While I am here, I plan to do what I came to do, including understanding this shift toward one collective community connecting energetically in our human, 3D experience on this Earth. The new paradigm is the antithesis of war, carnage, hate, divisiveness, separateness, and my fear-infused disaster stories.

I am curious whether we are already starting to experience a shift in the consciousness of humans, and that we are, on some scale, recognizing we are connected energetically. The mantra of *The Three Musketeers* comes to mind: "All for one and one for all!" Regarding our energetic connection, I remember one afternoon several years ago when my mom was the local ice arena caretaker/Zamboni driver. She had climbed a ladder to change a light bulb high above the ice surface and fell. She fainted from the pain and recalled waking up with the coolness of the ice on her face; then she fainted again, then repeat, with no recollection of the number of times. My dad found her lying on the ice when he stopped by on his way home from work. No one knew what time the fall happened until my grandpa, her dad, said that he had a searing pain in his normally healthy knee that afternoon and could not get up from the sofa. That was at 2:00 p.m. My mom had a broken kneecap from the fall, the same side, and had to have surgery to replace it. An interesting coincidence, perhaps, but we surmised the accident happened at 2:00 p.m.

Common examples of what the guides refer to as oneness or *we consciousness* is when we think of someone and the phone rings or when we have a conversation with someone and instantly feel a reciprocated warmth, connected and energized. Then we have the endless reels on our phones showing people helping people, animals saving people, people saving animals, animals saving animals, random acts of kindness, and then the story of my six-year-old granddaughter asking her mom if she could *PLEASE!* give the homeless man near the drive-through window her cookie. And another granddaughter, at seven years old, sobbing, overcome with sadness at the memorial of a young man whom she had never met but felt deeply the collective grief of his family and friends.

Why have people told me days before they died that they were dying? Did they know? They had not been aware of serious illnesses. I panicked every time and gently brushed them off. I was uncomfortable. I wish I knew then what I know now; I would have listened and allowed time for them to share. Looking back, they had connected with me in a way they felt comfortable sharing the most significant life event, and I was not anywhere near that new paradigm space to be present in a more meaningful way.

The *I consciousness* is keenly felt through our five senses as we maneuver through our day-to-day lives. Stuff happens; we feel, see, and react to it. We are victims of everything that happens to us; we are powerless. And it is not just outside of us, we are conflicted inside as well, unsure of who we are, with feelings of insecurity, unworthiness, and separateness. None of that sounds like good news especially when it is big stuff like serious illness, death, war, natural disasters, and the like. How do these things happen "for us" or "because of us"? I can see how some of our choices cause our illnesses and even death, but childhood neglect or serious childhood illnesses, not so much! Or were these choices somehow decided before we were born? Who would do such a thing? Were these the experiences our energy or soul selves chose to have in this lifetime? How many of the general population would buy that? It would probably take most people some serious soul searching to find the so-called gift in these tragedies.

As the guides explain, the new paradigm is the *we consciousness*. The word *consciousness* has been, in my mind, a woo-woo word connected to a lot of weird stuff, so I had to reframe it in a more pragmatic, real-life way. Consciousness is just being aware or more conscious of something. So, the *we consciousness* or the new paradigm is us being more aware that we are connected, sort of how we feel when we watch *We Are The World: The Story Behind The Song* and remember how we felt when that single raised over $60 million for African famine relief.

The new paradigm is *no separation*, and even though our five senses feel, see, touch, taste, and smell it, we can expand beyond them and perceive how our thoughts, feelings, and actions create what happens for us and because of us, and in doing so, take our power back, right? But since I struggle with certainty, even though I can articulate the guide's explanations, I am very aware as I sit in the present moment doing so, I am realizing my conceptualizing is not experiencing. I am new to the new paradigm, and I am gently moving forward with more understanding and less fear.

Contrary to my initial reaction, the new paradigm sounds much better than what we have experienced in our history and the challenges we are currently seeing around us. There are examples of how our energy expands toward a collective coming together in loving-kindness. These sweet sprinkles seem sparse compared to the discord in the political world, in the divisiveness surrounding religion, and in the treatment of minorities and anyone different from mainstream society. Is this just one last burst of the old paradigm before we see who and what we are to each other?

This Active Connection is complex from my understanding. I am curious how we will learn to perceive ourselves differently. Is it already happening? Will it happen gradually, with people gently expanding one by one, having a ripple effect around the globe? Will the lights go on suddenly, allowing us to see our individual selves melded into one energy? Or will we acutely remember that we are all part of this one energy source? I look forward to satisfying further curiosities and finding a deeper understanding of the new paradigm because this collective expansion or shift into a higher energetic frequency seems more and more like the whole point.

Vince and Mary's Reflections

This is the first session where the new paradigm is discussed. The evolution that is shared is energetic and/or spiritual. A movement toward all of us realizing we are one seems so important, yet so far away. When guidance is shared that we must accept knowing, living, and being all one, which is basically the new paradigm, we see the challenge in ourselves, let alone the whole of the collective, moving toward that consciousness. We are ready and willing. But are we able?

It actually feels empowering that we move from one stage of our humanity to the next. There is a trackable evolution, yet nothing is predetermined. When guidance talks about the *I consciousness*, it is easy to see the separation and the duality. Our society seems to be built on *mine* and *yours*. There is a need and a desire for us to move into the *we consciousness*. It is calming to know we are moving in that direction, although it is hard to accept with the disruption we see in the world.

At the same time, it can be troubling to think of each of us as separated and the evolution that must happen in us individually toward internal unity—bringing all parts of ourselves together with no separation from the outside to the inside.

Michele's reference to 2027 concerns the collective vibration on Earth being more aligned with the we consciousness than the I consciousness. This isn't to say the world would be different at that moment, but the energy shift would support faster transformation. This movement has been in the making for years. It takes more and more people answering their callings and being willing to move into the higher vibration of this consciousness to create this shift. Once the shift happens, we believe the movement toward the we consciousness will accelerate. We can participate in this transformation by learning to love all parts of ourselves. It is the transformation in each individual that facilitates the transformation of the collective.

Michele also shares the fear many of us have: the fear of the unknown. Generation after generation has justified this fear. The need to know or control keeps us stuck. We are unable to move toward a new way when we are afraid to leave the old way. Our future of living fully the reason we chose to come to Earth, can only come from living a new way. We must step beyond the limitations of the known and into the possibilities of the unknown.

Michele ends her musings with some powerful questions we can all ask ourselves. The answers will help us move further into the unknown.

Introspective Insights:
(Take a few minutes to journal or meditate on the following questions.)

1. Are there parts of you that you haven't accepted that create a separation in you?
2. How would it be more empowering for you to live from a oneness mindset?
3. Where has perceived separation caused disruption and resistance in your life?
4. How has the fear of the unknown kept you stuck in the trap of staying the same?

Expansion
(AC 3 Jan 24)

Each of you is on your planet to expand beyond what is even imaginable to your human mind. This expansion is not only experienced by you but will also be experienced by those around you and everyone you have ever come into contact with. All in support of the expansion of all that is.

The Round Table, channeled by Vince Kramer

There is much going on in the world, and yet we still are stuck in our old ways. What can you share?

> It is as it was planned to be. As you know, your world is but a small piece of the overall vastness of all there is. You, your world, and all there is coming together to experience the expansion of the whole. Each plane is a vital part of that expansion, each receiving the benefits of that expansion.
>
> There are many limitations that have necessarily been created over the eons of time to position your Earth, other planets, and the entire Universe to just where it is in this moment and the next moment and the next. All has been purposely designed to culminate in a new vibration. That expansion never ends. Each of

you in the third and fourth dimensions contributes to that expansion in every other dimension supporting you.

All are orchestrated by one conductor. That is the orchestra, the ball, the chairs, and everything—you are part of that conductor, and the conductor is you. Each of you on your Earth has the power of that conductor to orchestrate your life to be in alignment with and contribute to this concert you call life, and we call existence.

We are all one and destined by design to support expansion. Why do we look at our reason for being and what it means to expand so differently?

It takes every thought and understanding to expand the wholeness that is everything. Each of you chooses a different journey and path. So, the combination of all the pieces culminates in support of every aspect of universal expansion, which is made up of the sum of all the parts.

What you would call holistic is that it takes every belief, every bit of dogma, and every understanding of every concept to expand the whole. What you are really asking is who is correct and who is wrong in their beliefs about growth, alignment, enlightenment, and so on and so forth. And the answer, as you know it to be, is everyone is right, and no one is wrong. Each contributes to the whole, which is everything, all things.

It takes those who believe what they believe in, opening the avenue of growth and expansion to those who are looking for specific information and guidance at that moment. So you also know, that creates a new knowingness and expanded understanding. This is a constant cycle of moving toward the wholeness and magnificence of all there is.

Know that enlightenment, ascension, or any other concept that is bantered around doesn't look or show up in any one way; it presents itself in the way that best supports those in proximity to the energies. This is a constant and continuous set of interactions that are well-planned and well-orchestrated to support you all in your journeys and in your timing as you move toward having your Divine Intent, living your Divine Intent so others can live theirs, each living their personal version of enlightenment in every moment, and experiencing their ascension into the fullness of their energy stream.

In this now, Namaste.

Michele's Musings

This Active Connection expands on the concept of *expansion*. There is a grand perspective or picture of the entire Universe and our part to play in a new vibration. It had always bothered me that every human being had chosen a different journey. I never saw the benefit of the diversity of belief systems. I wanted there to be one, agreed upon by all, and for that one to be mine. Something inside me *needed* conformity or consensus, with at least some basic common ways of seeing the world. How could there *not* be a right and a wrong? Who is correct? According to this Active Connection, the whole point is the combination of every belief system in contributing, and therefore expanding, the whole. Well, that is a lot to digest!

If there was one way, I spent decades determined to find it. But the guides have a very different perspective: Everyone living their own personal versions of growth, alignment, enlightenment, ascension, or expansion.

I was conditioned to be "right" by my family dynamics, my religious beliefs, society, media, etc. I had wanted to be doing things the "right" way so badly that I contemplated being a nun when I was an adolescent. I loved the nuns! I loved the smell of homemade soup in the convent when I visited. I wanted to eat their food; they had bananas, which were a rare treat in my home, and they had the best cookies!

I loved how creative they were, and I watched them drawing and cutting with creative hands that were so white and clean. I learned how to play the guitar in the convent. I tried on the head covering one day and then made homemade ones to wear when I was alone. I made communion hosts by cutting carrots and officiating pretend church services with any of my six brothers who wanted to share in the excitement. I loved the smell of incense in the church and the stained glass windows. What I loved the most was knowing that I was in the *right* place, knowing the *right* things to do to get to heaven, and I was grateful that I was not one of the scary kids at the public school across the road—those unfortunate kids, most likely headed for hell.

A nun who taught typing class would hit our knuckles with a yardstick if we did not use the proper fingers to hit each key. It was a quick way to learn. If there is, in fact, a gift in every painful experience, the gift in the yardstick pain was the ability to type efficiently in my career and in my writing projects. I did not love the pain, but I loved it when some of the nuns treated me special. I was a good girl. I followed the rules. I did not, however, get the calling from God that would solidify a future in the convent and a sure way to heaven. What I did get was a rather intense discovery of boys, cute boys, boys who thought I was cute. With that came a world of sin and a fast-track to hell. The fear- and shame-based conditioning were reinforced for decades.

It is interesting that I stayed stuck in these old beliefs for most of my life. They seemed to be woven into my body, surfacing in irrational fears, a need to control situations and others, excess pressure, and harsh judgment of myself through the years. Avoiding rejection at any cost felt like a necessity for survival. I was able to see myself only through the perspectives of approval or disapproval from others.

This new energetic vibration the guides shared through Vince was intriguing and attractive. But how could I unravel the long-held beliefs that continued to limit my ability to move toward who I came here to be? And how could we move toward a sort of kumbaya oneness if we were all in different places energetically? Would we not have to be on the same page regarding our beliefs about growth and expansion to make this transition inside and outside of us? How would we be able to connect with each other in a real sense and transform how we maneuvered together on Earth in a heart-based, *we* perspective? I was drawn to this way of seeing things, this new paradigm, and the benefits of expansion, but I was not yet able to envision the grand plan. How could we ever get from here to there?

The guides share a new holistic perspective that it takes every belief, every bit of dogma, and every understanding of every concept to expand the whole. Nothing is "wrong"! Wherever we are, we are here to raise our own energy frequency and continue to expand our own energy, and each of us helps the other in this process. As they broke it down, it did not sound like a pie-in-the-sky idea, an unattainable goal, just a process of loving-kindness toward ourselves and others, a release of the old ways of seeing ourselves and realizing fully who we came here to be. I realized, though, that I still had significant resistance to embracing this idea that there is no right or wrong. But what I did appreciate was the inclusiveness of needing everyone in the process of expanding, no matter the belief system or where we were on our paths.

Vince and Mary's Reflections

This Active Connection session starts off quite deep. We are but a small part of the vastness of the Universe, yet we are a part of the conductor, and the conductor is us. This is hard to digest and absorb. It makes sense, but still, what does it mean? There is one energy, and we are all part of that energy. As such, we are that energy and here on the Earth to expand it. Fascinating!

It continues to be very deep in explaining the importance of every single thing, every similarity and every difference, for everything and everyone to function as designed. This is what they mean: There are no mistakes or coincidences. Everything is just as it is meant to be. We are all living the way we chose to support this expansion they talk about. We are meant to be just as we are as we go through expansion. It is easy to appreciate and yet so difficult to accept the simplicity and complexity simultaneously.

Michele shares her need to be right, which really translates into a need to be safe. How can we be safe if we don't have all the rules? If we are all the same and believe the same things, we know the rules, and we are safe. But there is no expansion in safety. In fact, safety is stagnation. It makes sense then that what guidance shares is that everything, everyone, and every way is needed. This is challenging because it pushes on basic human needs.

Michele illustrates how these rules keep us the same. But we are constantly being pulled to live one of the most important reasons to come to Earth: expansion. There are many reasons we resist expansion. The biggest is that we don't know what to expect in the unknown. It isn't safe. The questions she asks are the ones we all contemplate as we are asked to step into a new way. That new way is calling to us, and we can't help but step into it eventually.

Introspective Insights:
(Take a few minutes to journal or meditate on the following questions.)

1. What does it mean to you that we are all one energy?
2. What challenges does the statement "You are part of that conductor, and the conductor is you" pose for you?
3. Where are you reliant on being safe and willing to choose rules that limit you to being safe?
4. When do you resist experiencing the highest and lowest vibration when expanding?

Divine Intent
(AC 17 Jan 24)

Before your birth, as an integral part of source energy, you chose the streams of energy you would represent in your existence in the third dimension on your Earth. Then, you chose how you would make a difference, your reason for being. This is called your Divine Intent.

The Round Table, channeled by Vince Kramer

You have shared before about the concept of Divine Intent and making our difference. It is a challenge at times because of expected results. Can you help me understand?

> We would cherish this opportunity to help you see and feel through the understanding of this question. Your Divine Intent is your chosen mission. We, your Higher Self and the physical part of you, didn't *accept* that mission. We actually chose it. We understood exactly what living that mission would entail. We understood what was going to happen for us to learn every aspect of delivering the mission and the co-creations that would be needed to deliver it fully.

We even knew the trajectory and the possible results of living it. And we chose to live that life anyway. It is the life you and we call the "life you are meant to live." At your birth, you still knew and remembered all that knowingness. But there was a need to forget so that you could experience all the circumstances to help you learn and prepare to live your Divine Intent.

After you have experienced and developed enough to begin to live your reason for being on Earth and make that difference, it is time to start remembering what you forgot. We, your Higher Self and your guides, begin asking you to wake to this knowingness and your Divine Intent. Very basically, we are nudging you to begin to remember. For some, remembering starts very fast, and for others, it takes more time or messages before they pay attention to this request to wake up. These are what you describe as wake-up calls, and we can explain more about those in the future.

Most humans go through a process over years to start remembering. Each of you remembers more and more over time, but many never remember fully.

Yes, I understand all this. Can you share with me what it fully means to live your Divine Intent? I feel like I can only live it so far because it concerns others.

Living your Divine Intent entails remembering the real reason you came to Earth, uncovering your Unique Purpose, and remembering your Unique Purpose fully. Then, use all of your developed gifts and natural talents to create, recognize, and show up completely, for every opportunity to make your difference in the world. Remember that living your Divine Intent is you sharing your Unique Purpose to the highest possible level you can in each co-created circumstance.

It is about you choosing all your tools. This is about you living in your highest vibration as you share the real and concentrated essence of you. And last, it is you raising your vibration even higher in the act of delivering your gifts and talents and making your difference to the people whom you attract. No, that doesn't mean you will get the reaction that you want from the people you attract. Living your purpose fully doesn't mean that even though they were and are attracted to what you have to offer, they will be willing to fully or even partially remember their reason or difference. You are not responsible for their part in the co-creation they have with you. You must be willing to live *your* Divine Intent in that circumstance. Share your gifts and talents fully, see that you have lived your Divine Intent fully, and allow the expansion that you've created. And you must allow others to live their choice. You must allow them to stay the same if they choose and accept them if they decide to awaken or not.

You don't need the change in them to have lived your Divine Intent. We ask you to embody this and be willing to allow them to experience their co-creation with you and live how they choose, knowing that you are living your Unique Purpose. No matter what they choose, the joy must be on the inside of you and not dependent on the outside.

In this now, Namaste.

Michele's Musings

My chosen mission… I wish I had known this before reaching sixty years old. It felt like being a little late to the party! Perhaps this insight would have been helpful before beginning four years of university and a lengthy career.

When I was in high school, I was just going about my business on autopilot, fulfilling the expectations of others to succeed at something, anything. I was oblivious to any master plan that I had chosen before birth. I was awarded a volleyball scholarship to attend college in another province. That meant I would have to pick a major at seventeen when I had no idea what I wanted to be when I grew up. I was terrified of moving to a vast city, knowing only an aunt and uncle and the in-laws of a family member where I would live. I felt homesick whenever I saw *Little House on the Prairie* on one of my few television channels. My childhood home life was not quite the made-for-TV love and light of the home warmed by Ma and Pa Ingalls, but I missed being surrounded by familiar faces and familiar, simpler surroundings. I was moving to a sea of strangers in a busy, foreign city.

I was quickly immersed in college life, volleyball practices, tournament travel, parties, and a part-time job. It was late fall, early in the school year, when I walked forty minutes to campus one morning. I noticed something in the grassy median ahead of me between the two streets. It was a body—a woman's body. There was no such thing as cell phones, or I would have dialed 911. I walked a little closer to see if she was alive. It did not look like there was any movement. Her purse was lying on the ground beside her. I could not see any blood, but I did not get too close. I turned and ran back to the house and called the police. I sat for a few minutes, then started my walk to school again.

Not realizing it at the time, I was in shock. The day of classes was a thick fog and a waste of time, but at least I was not alone. I was too young, too immature emotionally, to be so far from home, to be starting on a career path that I fell into with the scholarship opportunity. *Or did I just fall into it?* Were these chosen experiences planned before I was born? Had I not honed my volleyball skills in school, I would not have gotten the scholarship, then I would not have started an education in corrections, and I would not have had a career in corrections and addiction treatment. I would not have been trained to help people to empower themselves and change their behavior.

That all sounds simple, but it was not, as there were many bumps—what I called mistakes, missteps, failing, getting back up, succeeding, and failing again. Was I already living my Divine Intent through these deeply muddy decades? The advantage of six decades of maturity is circling back and recognizing that it brought me where I am today. Were they mistakes or challenging rest areas on the map—challenging but purposeful places to recalibrate?

In my experience over the past several years, one of the biggest questions for people has been, "What is my purpose?" We are first curious about whether we have one, then if we believe we do, what is it? What if we were told it all at the beginning? There would be no experiences, no learning and growing, no contrast, no exploring, no adventures. What would be the point? And *is* there a point?

I was first introduced to the concept of Divine Intent while participating in the Take a Quantum Leap program with Vince and Mary. I learned that there are three parts to our purpose: quintessence, gift, and Divine Intent. And that uncovering these parts is remembering why we chose to be here. There is a grander mission or purpose in living this life on Earth. I found this prospect exciting, then overwhelming… had I already lived it? If I had not, was I too old to start living it now? I was still tired from my career, so now, how hard would living my purpose be? Could I do it? Did I want to? What if I knew it but chose *not* to live it? Then what?

During the program, I learned that I have an energy that radiates out and is felt by others. I had already believed we exude energy, as I can feel it from others when I enter a room; I had just not conceptualized it before. This energy is my quintessence, similar to essence but more refined. My specific quintessence is *focused support*. This surfaced during the exercises and was confirmed by feedback from a dozen close family and friends when I asked each about the energy they feel when they are with me.

My gifts and talents included a list from my education, training, life experiences, and career. So, my quintessence of *focused support* shines out into the world as I share and use my gifts and talents to fulfill my Divine Intent of *empowering others*.

Referring to Vince's question, the idea of making a difference at first glance had some scent of arrogance or grandiosity. Who are we to say we can make a difference and then whether, in fact, we have or not? I had found it off-putting when various New Agers perceived everyone needing the fixing they were selling. They were convinced they were changing (or saving) the world, one person at a time, while enjoying rather abundant fruits of their labor. Again, this is an old message alluding to saving us. But from what? Is *making a difference* referring to raising the frequency of ourselves, assisting others in doing the same, and together expanding the energy of the Universe? In a pragmatic sense, what would that look like day-to-day? How would it involve connections and interactions with others? For me, is it through sharing stories with people? Through my writing?

It was an interesting process to experience the unfolding of my Divine Intent, how I had already been doing some of it, and how I could ramp it up at sixty with a deliberate focus. Another part of the learning experience in Take a Quantum Leap that I appreciated was not just the focus on what we are good at in our gifts and talents but what we *love* to do. It did not have to be a job that I begrudgingly slogged at. I love to write. Could that actually be a part of it, to continue living my Divine Intent through my writing? Then I guess I *am* doing it, or at least making a valiant attempt to do so.

So, the guidance in this Active Connection goes even further: It is not enough to know your Unique Purpose, live it, and do what you are good at and love to do; it is about doing so in the highest energetic vibration. Whatever I do that is aligned with my purpose will potentially make a difference in the lives of the people who choose to receive it. There will be those attracted to what I share through my energy of *focused support* (my quintessence) as I use my gifts and talents to support them in empowering themselves. The caveat, though, related to Vince's question about knowing we are getting results and that we are making a difference, is that I am not responsible for whether they dig it or not.

It is a gentle invitation for me to live fully my Unique Purpose, and others have the choice to regard or disregard the purpose they came to live. Flying on autopilot or living unconsciously is comfy; it is the status quo, the mainstream. I enjoyed it there, until I didn't. I had felt in my bones that there was more. My incessant curiosity did not kill the cat! Deep down, I felt I was here for more, and I had to find what that was. Even in this short time of learning and remembering my Divine Intent, I gave up many times, reverted to old beliefs, got lazy, and stagnated. I did not want to risk being wrong AGAIN! I did not want to risk being different, being out of the weirdo closet, or being rejected.

Eventually, I completed the class, framed my Unique Blueprint, and started recognizing where and how I was, in fact, using my gifts and talents, shining my little light out into the world, fulfilling my Divine Intent day-to-day in my connections and interactions with people in my periphery. I chose to consider and accept opportunities that aligned with my purpose in this life. It is nothing grandiose or arrogant. Rather, it felt like wearing a shoe that does not fit if I chose not to act in service of the larger picture, the expanding of the Universe's energy, and, ultimately, the movement toward the new paradigm. Really, it is just me, transforming my perception, consciously and thoughtfully raising my energetic frequency, living my Divine Intent, each day maneuvering from that simple, humble space.

Vince and Mary's Reflections

This Active Connection explains that we are truly on Earth to live on purpose. We chose this experience at every dimension, knowing what it would look like to live our reason for being. We chose it at a multidimensional level, and both the physical and nonphysical parts of us work together to live it fully. They share that our reason for being, the difference we are here to make, is our Divine Intent. It is our why, as we have heard it called. It is only one of the three parts of our Unique Purpose. The reminder that as we develop all that we need to make that difference, it is time to wake up. It is important to note the reminder guidance shared with us that we are responsible for living our Divine Intent. We aren't responsible for any outcome or lack of outcome experienced by anyone else. This gives us great personal responsibility and, at the same time, removes us from any responsibility for external outcomes. You are here to live your Divine Intent.

As Michele points out, we all wish we had known our purpose, our Divine Intent, earlier in life. As the guidance points out, we did. We just didn't remember. Our hope is that as this information gets more widely accepted, we will be able to help people discover their Divine Intents earlier in life. This will help us make more aligned life decisions, as Michele suggested. We want you to understand that not knowing your Divine Intent is not keeping you from moving closer to it or living it at least somewhat. Once you know it and can define it, you will see you have been living it all along.

Michele asks if she was living her Divine Intent through the muddy decades. Our answer to her is yes. Everything in our lives are creations and co-creations that lead us somehow, making the biggest difference possible. You might be learning a new skill, experiencing a new emotion, or learning to support yourself or others. All of these lead you to being the best and most effective you. It doesn't matter if it is something you chose before you were born or created in that now moment; it will serve you in being you and living your Divine Intent. Don't get wrapped up in why it happened and pay attention to the gift. As Michele illustrated so well, everything truly does happen for a reason.

What is my purpose? This is a very popular question. In fact, the two most asked questions in the world are: Who am I? and, Why am I here? Your Unique Purpose is actually the who, what, and why of you. We all have one. You just need to find your answers. When you learn how to find your answer, you can start living your Divine Intent fully. It is never too late. Ever!

The three parts of your purpose, in combination, are unique to you. They make you special but no more unique or special than anyone else.

> **Introspective Insights:**
> (Take a few minutes to journal or meditate on the following questions.)
> 1. Describe the who, what, and why of you.
> 2. What are the times in your life that you wonder why they happened?
> 3. What would your life be like if you knew your Divine Intent?
> 4. How do you think you may already be living your Divine Intent?

Not Believing
(AC 5 Feb 24)

After choosing your reason for incarnating on the Earth plane as a strand of universal energy, you chose your parents and grandparents to help you learn and experience the circumstances and develop the beliefs that will help you become all you are meant to be to live the reason you chose fully.

The Round Table, channeled by Vince Kramer

You talk about what is coming with the new paradigm and the change that we all must go through. What if someone doesn't believe that this guidance is real or important?

> That is an excellent question with many answers. Let us look at the human experience. We have shared with you that you have always been getting guidance. This guidance is increasing and becoming more visible to you. There is movement in people on your planet learning how to get their guidance in ways like Active Connection. It is an essential part of moving into this new paradigm we speak of. It is a shift, not just for you but for the majority of those on your planet. It challenges old beliefs and raises old stigmas, just in getting guidance, talking to the angels and masters, if you will.

This takes a leap of faith and requires trust. And this leap of faith will be easy for some and not so easy for many. At this now moment, many won't believe it because they have been taught that it isn't real, not possible, or even that they are crazy if they hear or get this guidance. The collective of your world also believes if it doesn't come from your brain that it is not real. Couple this with the belief that it is not real if not experienced by the five senses, and it leaves people feeling that they are just making it up. When they do get guidance, the human experience comes with free will. You all can choose to believe or not believe, to trust or not, and to follow this guidance or not.

Those who choose to receive this guidance will get it freely. Those who don't will get it in many ways, but they still have the choice not to believe it or accept it. Some will get the guidance but not trust it or choose not to take action on it. That all is free will. These people will stay the same. There will be little or no growth. Their vibration or frequency will stay the same.

This will not be an issue for them at first. Still, as more and more begin to get, accept, and follow the guidance they receive, the vibration of the collective will rise, and this will cause those who have chosen through their free will not to follow the guidance or even believe in it to experience incoherence. This will create chaos in their lives. They will feel they don't belong. If they continue not to receive, follow, and trust guidance, the gap in their vibration will cause them to feel alone, unseen, and out of touch. This change of vibration will be difficult for them to be in or around.

Many of these people will choose to leave the planet. We are not suggesting suicide, although some may choose to leave in that manner. We are seeing that the nonphysical part of these people will choose to create or co-create circumstances that will result in death. This could and can be an illness or disease caused by the low vibration the person is experiencing. It could be an accident or just not waking up one morning. This is not a punishment or anything like that. It is the vibrational changes of energy that are happening and coming in the shift in the paradigm we have shared.

You all are being guided, whether you accept it or not, to move into this high vibration. Some will leave your planet as they complete their chosen journey on it. Some will leave because they chose not to trust and follow guidance, and some will leave because they chose not to believe in guidance, all in divine order, with their choice in exercising their free will. Others will move into the higher vibration of the new paradigm and support the movement from the *I consciousness* to the *we consciousness*.

In this now, believe, trust, and expand into who you are meant to be. Namaste.

Michele's Musings

Why did I find this Active Connection so triggering? First, I am one of the people, as the guides mention, who finds it difficult to trust guidance. I believe it is there, so that is handy, and it is not like I do not trust it all, but the trust is sporadic. More about that later. Second is the fear that surfaced with the Active Connection. I can choose to believe the new paradigm is unfolding and sort of be okay with it, and then there are days that I contract in fear, doubt, and skepticism. Perhaps it is the abstractness of it. I have not yet heard it explained specifically how my day-to-day life will change. What is actually coming? Perhaps I have not understood it yet. Maybe I am just not ready. So, at this point of vague understanding, my mind goes as is programmed, to the worst-case scenario, a disaster story. I erroneously read between the lines and reacted accordingly. Add to that, a year ago, I saw a preview on the television for *Heaven's Gate: The Cult of Cults*. I could not imagine the level of gullibility. That may sound a bit strange, coming from someone who is not only learning to believe and trust channeled messages from Vince's nonphysical guides but writing about it!

Initially, I was curious, as there was actual footage of interviews of cult members and former members; it was the largest mass suicide on US soil. I was intrigued and a little shocked by the language in the short clip. It was eerily familiar with the language I had heard during the few years on the New Age train. I watched the short series. OMG! This was the same language! Was I believing in similar messages that were dressed up as recycled New Age?

It freaked me out a bit! I had been listening to various New Age followers and teachers who were excitedly discussing ascension and how to hop on the bus. This language about preparing for the big shift included, "Hurry, it's coming!" and "You don't want to miss it!" and "You must disconnect from your family if they do not get on board." The Heaven's Gate leader's language was inflated, but the nuance was similar. Some of the cult enticements and endorsements included being the holder of the *real* truth, being special and belonging with other true believers, overcoming or transcending humanness, preparing for the end of Earth or at least Earth as we know it, being the chosen, awakened, enlightened ones, etc. For them, believing involved leaving belongings and family behind and, ultimately, their human existence.

I understood the enticement, especially looking back at challenging times in my life. Still, I found it disturbing that people were susceptible to being preyed upon despite being intelligent and educated. They were seemingly desperate people, desperate to believe, trust, and surrender. They went all in and were convinced to such an extreme that they chose to leave their physical lives. I witnessed how they prepared with anticipation and excitement, equivalent to planning for a sunny getaway in the Caribbean. Unfortunately, but understandably, stories like this repel people from believing or trusting even science-based nonphysical guidance.

Now, how does any of this relate to the Active Connection and our guidance? Our beliefs, although not real, as the guides have explained, can be so powerful and can catapult us in strange directions, especially when we hang on tightly. They reveal our human fragility and our human strength. I choose to believe in this new paradigm process, or I would not be writing about it. I believe that we are energy, that everything is energy because our current science proves it. And as energy beings, from day-to-day, moment to moment, we choose higher frequency energetic states or lower ones. Energy never ends; it is not static; it expands or contracts. Our guides, Trusted Source, and nonphysical support are all energy, and it is all coming from the main energy generator of sorts that we are a part of, that is us.

This is not about metaphysics or being special or chosen by an omnipotent being or aliens; it is about science and humans as 3D physical beings, as part of the nonphysical support that cannot *not* be connected to us. I relate it back to *The Matrix*, plugging into the energetics of the Universe. Being awake in this sense is just being aware that even though we are living a 3D human existence, our essence fundamentally is energy.

But change can still be unsettling, and there is that niggling fear around the shift or transformation into expanded energy and what that means. And I do not consistently trust my own guidance. I must mention, though, that it is interesting that so far, when the guides have referred to the paradigm shift, they have never ever mentioned the global mayhem or disaster I envisioned, not once. They have mentioned numerous times a movement toward higher energetic frequencies of connection, community, *we consciousness*, and oneness, so why the trepidation? For me, resistance is most likely the result of long-held beliefs, that not-so-little voice in our heads, the old systems of beliefs similar to religious cults, and religious biblical accounts of global disaster in Revelations. But there is hope.

This is where I have found that the Active Connection, or other ways in which we choose to receive nonphysical guidance and support, is so important. I have realized through this process, and gratefully so, that we are always getting guidance, whether we believe it or not or trust it or not. We call it our intuition, our gut sense, our spider sense, the cute angel or devil on our shoulders, or just a knowingness that suspends logic or understanding. It took an unimaginable occurrence to shake my untrusting nature to the core, but that's a wild story for another day.

In the meantime, my belief is evolving; there is no dreadful disaster story to fear. I am letting go of that belief gently and gradually. I understand, at least conceptually, that the expansion of the energy of the Universe is something to invite and embrace and for us to participate in as energetic beings in our higher frequency emotional and energetic states. The rest for me personally can be felt sweetly smoldering and transforming within me as I enjoy this co-creative process. Besides, as explained, the energetic shift is already happening, even though there is much separation in our society. The evidence of oneness may seem sparse and distant. Still, as mentioned in other chapters, this separateness is part of the process and only an indication that we are in the progression of expanding and moving toward a new paradigm, our happy place, so to speak.

Vince and Mary's Reflections

One of the most empowering parts of this guidance is that we are all constantly getting guidance. We just need to know how to hear it. It was refreshing to learn that more and more of us are learning to get it in a useful way. The next concern is when we will start following it or taking action on it. We have to be willing to take the leap of faith that they talked about. It is a willingness to follow your heart.

The emphasis on living in a world of choice was important. But we are also happy to know that even if you choose not to hear or pay attention to your messages, you are still going to get them, and someday, you will wake up to them. We have heard of wake-up calls many times before. There is a choice around wake-up calls also. If we refuse to wake up, basically, our time on Earth is complete. It sounds harsh that our higher selves might take us out. But is there a reason to stay? It is comforting to know we aren't alone. We are being guided.

Michele shares that there is a lack of security in this message. She is uncomfortable with something she doesn't understand. The fear comes from that lack of understanding. She shared that in her discomfort, her mind goes to old beliefs. Not knowing what life might look like becomes a wall separating her from the possibilities. It is interesting that it leads her to cults. The guidance in this book has never been to convince you of something you refuse to believe. It has been to open you to new possibilities. It is our old beliefs and fears that pull us into the darkness. Nowhere is there talk of leaving anything or anyone behind. It is about finding and fully living every part of you. Although there have been discussions of vibration, people moving separate ways because of incoherence is much different from the cult example.

It is extremely important that we learn to tap into our own guidance and find our own way. It isn't about being enticed by someone else's life or way. It is about finding your way and having the courage to step into it. We highly recommend that you *don't* follow someone else's way. In fact, it would be best to avoid those who tell you their way is the right way.

Michele shares her experiences with tapping into guidance through Active Connection, and you can see the importance of finding your answers from the higher vibrational parts of you. That is where you will find the answers for you specifically. You are unique, and that requires you to find your unique answers.

Introspective Insights:
(Take a few minutes to journal or meditate on the following questions.)

1. When do you find it hardest to believe there might be more?
2. What beliefs and fears have you been given or have you chosen that might keep you stuck?
3. Where in the past have you been given guidance that you questioned or ignored?
4. What are the questions you would ask that all-knowing part of you after reading this chapter?

Believing
(AC 20 Jan 24)

You are constantly being supported by the higher vibrations of your chosen energy stream(s). Guidance is being shared in messages and promptings. These messages and promptings come in all shapes and sizes and are always trying to get your attention. You choose whether or not you look for them, whether or not you listen to them, and whether or not you take action on them.

The Round Table, channeled by Vince Kramer

I have often considered this question because I was disbelieving when I first started paying attention to messages in my life. What if we don't believe we can get or are getting information or guidance?

> This is a good question, and it has answers at many levels. Let's begin with the understanding that each of you has access to all the information and knowledge and can and have been benefiting from it even if you don't believe you can get it. Also, we want you to know that when you were born, it wasn't like there was a light switch or, maybe more appropriately, a radio switch that you or someone else turned off so you could no longer tap into or hear this guidance.

Through your earliest years in this incarnation, you were connecting with and receiving guidance. You know this because your grandmother told you that you shared with her at an early age why you were on Earth. But most people on Earth forget and stop believing in this connection that they experienced as children—and still have. In knowing that there are no mistakes or coincidences in our Universe, we ask you to understand that this forgetting was the chosen journey of each person who forgets.

As we have shared, when it is time to wake up, your Higher Self will create the opportunity or, in most cases, the opportunities to choose to remember and once again believe that you have this connection to guidance, through the nonphysical part of you and the higher vibrations of your energy stream.

When we say that it is part of the journey, much has come from your forgetting, and forgetting was baked into your plan. The collective has moved away from believing that you have this access or that many deserve this access. Many have been taught that if they haven't forgotten, when they connect to this information—talking to the angels or spirits—there is something wrong with them or that they're bad. For those of you who maintained a connection or haven't been taught that you are wrong or bad, you have been taught that those people who believe they can connect are evil or crazy.

There are many reasons those who are in charge or want the best for you tell you and teach you these beliefs, but they are not relevant to this session or your question. What is pertinent is that even if you don't believe you can get your answers, your Higher Self is constantly trying to wake you up to understanding and, at the same time, creating circumstances to guide you toward being all you are meant to be, chose to be. For those who want to connect, reach out and ask your questions and expect answers because they are there for you.

Listen, watch, and notice because they are there. Don't hesitate to ask for a message to come in a way that you can't deny that message has come to you. The guides are higher vibrations of your energy stream and have a purpose to help you grow, expand, and experience the fullness of your energy stream.

They are constantly sending you messages and promptings not only to help you remember but to fully live your reason for choosing to come to your Earth. Know that your Higher Self will find a way to wake you up to give you proof that you can connect. It will continue to increase the volume of the message, if you will, until you *must* pay attention and can no longer deny your ability to connect to guidance or your uniqueness and your magnificence, and you will have no choice other than to believe.

In this now, Namaste.

Michele's Musings

As I contemplated this Active Connection, initially, an analogy of lacking connection came to mind. There was limited cell coverage when we began our time at the pristine Canadian prairie lake. We loved our small camper in the early days. It was simple and comfortable, and the lake view was lovely. Cell phones were old-school flip phones. To have cell coverage, we would stand on the picnic table. When we traded the little camper for what we deemed a luxurious, larger one with a master bedroom and bunk beds, we could stand in one specific corner, reach up high with the phone to our ear, and have coverage there.

Eventually, we traded up for a Park Model; now that was true luxury! There were still two bedrooms, but in this dwelling on wheels, we had cell coverage throughout. We could walk around either side of the bed and had a living room, small kitchen, and dining area. My research into nonphysical and connecting to guidance could be analogous to cell coverage. I had to move to higher ground (frequency) to have adequate coverage, and in doing so, the remembering began. I had connected to guidance during the Take a Quantum Leap program; I was sure of it at the time, asking questions, getting answers, and watching for messages and promptings, but then I slid back into autopilot. My Active Connections were real but, over time, became few and far between, and doubt seeped in. My subpersonalities took the wheel.

Then came an opportunity for another higher-ground experience: a retreat in Mount Shasta, California, a prime location to *remember the forgetting*. Would I feel the energy of the vortices? It was said that feeling it would be unavoidable. That would be cool! I wanted to feel connected with an immersive experience, away from daily ups and downs. I needed a space to connect again through Active Connection.

While visiting the sacred sites, I felt it. It was extraordinary and soothing and believable that we are all connected, that we are all energy, that we are NEVER alone, and that guidance is always there, more accurately, here inside us, no matter the names we give it. When I connected with the guides, it was the energy I experienced in Take a Quantum Leap Active Connection exercises, the energy streams of which my energy is a part. Ideally, my "cell coverage" is high-speed, a high frequency energy connection. As I remember it, my Higher Self is creating circumstances that are guiding me to be who I came here to be. I am so grateful to be experiencing this, and I truly believe it is available to everyone.

The guidance says we forget much of it when we are born, our matrix-like superpowers almost dormant from our psyches, but as young children, we still have some memory, then slowly it withers through conditioning. "It's just your imagination." "There's no such thing as invisible friends." "You're just being silly and childish." Soon, we have forgotten, and the belief that we are connected to constant guidance is no longer part of our experience, even though the guidance never leaves us. I love the guide's quote, "Forgetting was baked into your plan." Bumping along, learning, and growing and slowly (more quickly with significant wake-up calls), eventually remembering or choosing not to. So, if the planned power outage or amnesia continues throughout our lifetime, then what happens? Perhaps it goes on the shelf until the next lifetime?

In my perception, the new paradigm is remembering so we can get our guidance as we listen to messages and promptings. It is the freedom of being released from the cage of disempowering beliefs, exploring and experiencing who we are, why we are here, and living a dynamic, fulfilling life. The experience of the adventures inside an escape room comes to mind, unlocking the mysteries and excitedly solving the riddles to move forward. The new paradigm allows the remembering after the forgetting was baked into our plan. I experience freedom in the awareness of knowing who I really am and accepting, embracing, and loving who I was and am on the outside and, even more so, on the inside, especially through this growth process.

I acknowledge that through this waking-up work, I am more conscious than ever that it is my Higher Self, the higher frequency part of our shared energy stream, that is guiding me as I reach out regularly and expect answers through Active Connection. I also recognize guidance through relationships with other people, through books, through dreams, and even television shows and movies. I see my progress in transforming my perception of co-creating the life I continue to choose, and I appreciate learning through challenging and changing disempowering beliefs. I am learning to respect others no matter the path they are choosing. I am gradually increasing my remembering and solidifying my connection even on days when I struggle to surrender and trust it.

I love the support, encouragement, and hope in the Active Connections, and day-to-day, I choose to be more aware or conscious rather than maneuvering on autopilot. Imagine no longer being able to deny our uniqueness and magnificence! I am finally noticing and acting on the promptings or wake-up calls, starting to trust that guidance is not something I have to force or go looking for. It is an ever-constant companion, a part of me, the birthright of every human on this beautiful Earth.

Vince and Mary's Reflections

This guidance really enforces that we are on a journey that is well supported. It shares that we are constantly getting help and direction to help us live the life that we choose. We were especially intrigued by the fact that it was necessary for us to forget, but in forgetting, we also disconnected from this guidance. As we look back now, we can see these messages or promptings they talk about. They were things that I might have considered a synchronicity, serendipitous, or even worse, happenstance. We definitely treated many, if not most, of them as coincidence at best. So many of us have been taught to trust our brains or our minds. We believe that the answer must come from there. There is safety in relying on our experience of the past to control our future.

I was also intrigued by the realization that the people who do maintain a level of connection have been made wrong or even categorized as something bad. This, in itself, had to be instrumental in many of us shutting down this connection. Refusing to listen because we would be perceived poorly or negatively was more than enough reason. We are encouraged by this message, hoping as you read it, you will be willing to be open to and receive guidance to support you. We hope you are also intrigued and will start watching and listening for the proof that these messages have been coming your way all along.

Michele reminds us how amazing it feels when we choose to believe. The connection with the all-knowing part of ourselves is all we really need to remember and then recognize ourselves fully. It has been shared through other Active Connections similar to the one above that the souls coming to the world at this time aren't forgetting. There is no need for them to forget. What that means is, they will need more of us to remember so we can support them.

Like Michele, we all have our concept of what it means to move into a new paradigm. And… there are no rights or wrongs. It's not the concept that is in question. It is, *Are we ready to fully step into this new paradigm and grow and expand as needed to be all we can be?*

Introspective Insights:
(Take a few minutes to journal or meditate on the following questions.)

1. Am I being called to listen to my guidance?
2. As I reflect back on my life, where were there messages that I ignored?
3. How can I develop a way or find a way to connect to guidance on a regular basis?
4. How would my life be different if I believed I could connect?

Roadblocks
(AC 19 Feb 24)

You have access to all the knowledge of the universe. Every idea ever had and every thought is available to you. You are supported by the higher vibrations every step of the journey you choose. All the obstacles in your way are internal and supported by your lower vibrations.

The Round Table, channeled by Vince Kramer

What are the biggest roadblocks to us believing our guidance and taking action?

> There are many roadblocks as diverse as those who doubt their guidance, as well as roadblocks for those who aren't doubting. We will share many of the common ones with you. As you have heard from us many times, the roadblocks are all on the inside, and they are beliefs that you have formed throughout your life, beliefs that have come from other people and ones that you formed on your own based on your perceptions of your circumstances and experiences of your life. Let us share some of the most common with you.

Many of the most common result from fear, which is a very low vibration, and in themselves can keep you from receiving guidance. There is the question in people's minds about whether or not they are worthy. Believing that these energies are so much better than they are, they ask themselves, Who am I to be able to talk to these guides? They let the belief of not being worthy stop them from connecting in any way. Another big belief that stops them is the fear of being alone. Many people are in relationships where their partner and or friends aren't ready to believe that they can access their guidance. Their partners and friends have their own beliefs that prevent them from tapping in. This leaves the person feeling that they will lose all the people in their lives and will be all alone. They also fear they will be ridiculed and put down.

There are still others they can't trust that are actually connected to the higher vibrations of their energy stream. They believe they are making up the answers they receive. This mistrust in themselves results in losing interest, and they never develop confidence in their connection. There are people who believe connecting with guidance in this way is wrong; even people who pray on a regular basis doubt that they can actually get answers and receive them in a way that they consider less than divine. Some have a belief that others can get guidance directly, but they aren't capable. The fear of failing keeps them from even trying to get started. They convince themselves it can't be done, many times without even trying.

These and less common beliefs have kept many from getting valuable guidance. We can tell you that as more people are willing to open themselves to their guidance and share their experiences with others, others will begin to accept the possibilities and open themselves to receiving their own guidance. They will begin to trust the messages and promptings given to them and move beyond the fears that they have built and nourished by taking on the beliefs of others. You all have access to all the knowledge of the Universe, and your guides, the angels, and the masters are waiting to share all the knowledge with you.

Move beyond the beliefs that limit you, know that you are worthy, you are good enough, and when you trust in your guidance, you will attract like-minded and like-hearted people into your life. You will never be alone. Trust in your guidance and your ability to connect.

In this now, Namaste.

Michele's Musings

Undeserving is one of the limiting beliefs that I have held near and dear. How can I deserve the ability to connect and the certainty of connection, with conditioning messages like stay humble, stay small, never acknowledge your innate abilities, or that guidance comes from us, from inside? And this is what limiting beliefs look like in real life; I react daily to outside occurrences. I have a specific idea of how I expect people to be, and I prefer that we are all on the same page, my page, always. I am not yet a good *accepter* of others and their paths. Another, if I am grateful for what I have, it will be taken away, and I probably did not deserve it in the first place.

Beliefs are interesting and fickle, a virtue to hold tightly, synonymous with a strong faith. Strong beliefs are especially perceived as true. I am learning this is not so. They are really just thoughts we think over and over. And they are not true. If they were, we would not be choosing to change them from one minute to the next or one year to the next. I am learning that our beliefs are the foundational motivation for our thoughts and everything we do, whether we are aware or not.

I believed some crazy stuff, initially related to religion, because that was my early lived experience and the foundation of many of my juiciest beliefs. Fear of hell was a biggie, as I mentioned in other chapters, as well as original sin, the revolving confessional door which felt terrifying, humiliating, and shaming, and also the belief that we do not have access to wisdom and knowledge about our own lives. The belief was that it must come from outside of us or can cost a lot (unless it is through authority figures of various religious institutions, in which case it is free monetary-wise, but costly in other ways).

I did not get a call from a loved one recently for a few weeks, which was very much out of the ordinary. I spiraled into "What did I do?" "Oh my God, I miss her! What if she doesn't talk to me anymore?" and all the way to "What if she leaves me?" I was so upset, I cried. One-word texts felt icy; I even tried the frowned-upon, live, phone call, but no answer. I tried to tell myself something different: *She is busy and stressed; it is not about me; and there are other things going on in her life.* I blamed the overreaction on the immune-suppressants I was taking. Apparently, steroids can cause extreme emotional states. I was already too upset to allow higher-frequency thought options to replace the irrational, upsetting ones. The low frequency of thoughts went on for a few more days, then subsequently, I had more days of not feeling connected to nonphysical source energy.

As it turned out, she had not left me; she was a busy, working mom with significant stressors, and I had just opted to spend more than a week in the basement of energetic frequency. And, of course, as I open myself to challenging the thoughts, the obstacles that often squeeze out trusting and receiving—limiting beliefs—surface like an endless smack of jellyfish floating gently to the surface in the ocean. (Fun fact: a group of jellyfish is called a *smack*!)

I have limited experience in believing and trusting my own guidance. I am also surrounded by people in my life who would or will see me as a kook for believing I can connect with nonphysical energy, whether I call them guides, masters, or even dicier, the *angelic* realm. That is a tough one! So, how can anyone be a vessel for supporting others in seeing the possibilities for the picking and the potential of a most desired, fulfilled life if the vessel is not perceived as credible, or worse?

I am among the increasing numbers who are mostly convinced that humans have access, especially since I have been experiencing the few trusted channelers, one being Vince. I admit that I also teeter on doubting but want to believe that I too am connecting. I want certainty! How easy is it to trust for those who communicate clearly with the energy of passed loved ones, for channelers who feel it, see it, and trust it, and for those who, from a young age, continue to see auras, angels, and an assortment of other fun nonphysical beings. I seek that luxury, to know without any doubt. That is the state we look forward to, the higher energetic frequency movement toward experiencing the new paradigm, spreading like warm lava and transforming the majority into an awake, peaceful, connected, and expanded state.

This one gives me hope: "The greater the doubt, the greater the awakening; the smaller the doubt, the smaller the awakening; no doubt, no awakening." C.C. Chang

If that is the case, I am in for a *huge* awakening! Imagine being awakened to our true selves as energy streams of nonphysical source energy, *the only source of energy*. And finally, trusting our connection with and access to this high frequency information and guidance for *everything*, all ours for the asking and receiving, dependent on our choice of energetic frequency. Conceptually, I understand it to a certain extent. Still, it is obvious that I trust nonphysical guidance through The Round Table more than I trust my own, especially for life's more significant questions and, to be honest, probably *most* questions. Practicing Active Connection regularly is promising, though, with a slow but gradual increase in trusting the guidance that surfaces when I tune in and write responses to questions. Some days, it takes a leap of trust when I question if I am imagining it; other days, I feel like I am truly connecting. It often depends on where my energy is during the day or where it is in the evening when I usually tune in.

I understand the fear the guides refer to in this Active Connection. I came out of the religious closet terrified of being banished but thankfully, mostly unscathed. When this project takes me out of the weirdo closet, will my loved ones leave me? Some may think that I have finally drunk the Kool-Aid and stepped off the deep end; perhaps they already do. For those closest, I expect some good-natured jeering or, a favorite in my witty family, a little sarcasm. So, yes, I still care what others think of me, and I wish to be perceived as somewhat intelligent, fun, "normal," and someone with interesting ideas and opinions. Will the limiting beliefs behind approval-seeking be roadblocks to connecting, especially if I react to criticism or strong opinions about myself or my writing? Imagine what they will think if I share what I say every morning, "Good morning, angels," and every night, "Thank you, angels." (I guess I just did.) I laughed to myself one night when I realized I was sounding like Charlie in the old television show *Charlie's Angels*.

This Active Connection shows I am the only one who can get in the way of trusting my connection and acting on it. The good news: We are always connected whether we are aware or not, and I am completely and solely responsible for the frequency of energy that I choose to hold in trusting the guidance. I also understand the roadblocks are mine to remove, like picking weeds in an overgrown garden. And if you know weeds, they are hardy and can be relentless, thriving no matter the conditions. But I am doing it; I am setting an intent every night of what I want my life to be, and I have seen results, especially in being conscious of my thoughts and of the energy that I put out every day in every circumstance and experience. I am less concerned about what others think, although personally, the belief around that one is a deeply rooted thistle.

It is cliché, yes, but it is progress not perfection, and the benefit of enjoying the early days of trusting that I am always connected to the nonphysical outweighs the work it requires to take a leap and be more conscious. It is the unfolding of the new paradigm.

Trusting this one and only energy source is us becoming, or rather returning to, our natural and whole state of being, of oneness.

Vince and Mary's Reflections

Much of the new paradigm work involves realizing that we are responsible for our lives. Mastering our minds is an essential part of living our lives on purpose. This guidance is very direct in stating that all the roadblocks to living our Unique Purpose are internal. It also states that all are associated with our individual belief systems. They leave no doubt on who is in control. We do not live a predetermined life. We follow our own set of rules either consciously or unconsciously. But they are not just roadblocks in living our lives fully; they also can stop us from getting guidance.

Fear and doubt can stop us from getting guidance, which makes even more sense when considering vibration. If guidance comes from a higher vibration, we must be in a higher vibration to receive it. As they pointed out, fear and doubt are low vibrations. Thus, they create the inability to receive guidance.

There are so many beliefs and rules around tapping into this higher vibrational knowledge. The most disturbing one is believing it is somehow wrong to get guidance. Societal and group beliefs, in many cases, make it evil or dubious. Those beliefs are based on fear of the unknown.

We all have the ability to tap into guidance if we trust and surrender. When you do, it doesn't take long before you realize you are getting information you have never heard before, and then you have no choice but to believe.

Michele shares the feeling of being undeserving of tapping into higher vibrational guidance. We find it disturbing that we have been taught or at least convinced that we don't deserve it. It shows the separation that has been created purposefully and otherwise. We are all Universal Energy. It is our birthright to have this guidance. It is time we are taught how to tap into this guidance.

Michele's circumstances are perfect examples of great times to reach out for guidance. Learning more about what is going on in your life can be extremely helpful in living a more empowered life. We tend to allow ourselves to be pulled back into the past and old ways of being. It is time we find a new way, our individual way.

The doubt Michele shares about getting unfiltered information from her trusted sources is typical. We have found that this mostly comes from fears. First, we are always afraid of being wrong. Second, we want to believe we are just making stuff up. I love helping people see that the guidance they are getting is something they would never say to themselves.

It all comes down to trusting and surrendering to the magic of who you are.

Introspective Insights:
(Take a few minutes to journal or meditate on the following questions.)

1. Where do you have beliefs that are keeping you from even attempting to get guidance?
2. Where do you worry about what others think?
3. What are your beliefs about losing people in your life because of what you believe?
4. How would your life be different if you trusted your guidance instead of the voices in your head that keep you stuck?

Meant for More
(AC 8 Feb 24)

You are Universal Energy living a third-dimension existence to fully experience the highest and lowest vibration of your energy stream(s). You are the creator of your life and capable of manifesting any and all of the unlimited possibilities available to you in the Universe. By design, you are meant for more, no matter where you are in any moment.

The Round Table, channeled by Vince Kramer

We seem to *not* want to believe we are meant for more, and we allow ourselves to accept what is. Can you help us understand why?

> Certainly. First, understand that there are no mistakes or coincidences. Everything you experience is divinely created by your Higher Self, that nonphysical part of you. This concept is the same for the macrocosm as it is for the microcosm of you.
>
> The culture of your society plays a big energetic part in your life. Especially if you don't choose to master your mind and move into the highest vibrations of yourself. There are three major limiting beliefs that are held by most humans and the collective as a whole.

They are, I am not good enough; I am not worthy; and I'm not lovable.

These beliefs are very limiting because they are proof to you that you don't deserve more than you have in this moment. These beliefs are reflected back to you in the relationships and circumstances you attract into your life through the Law of Attraction. In these attractions, you are proving to yourself that you aren't worthy, good enough, or lovable. You stop trying, moving, or creating more because you hold these beliefs. Your subpersonalities use these beliefs against you to encourage you not to move forward and possibly be heard or disappointed.

Many in your society have been taught by their parents or other influential grown-ups in their lives that it is okay not to be *more*. They prove through their rationalizing that not everyone can be rich, successful, or happy. They share these things believing that they are helping the person feel better about themselves or hoping they won't be disappointed. Others share their beliefs about society being rigged, that the playing field isn't level, and that there are people out to get you—people in the government, the rich, or everyone in general are out for themselves at your expense.

Know that, as we have shared with you before, beliefs aren't real. They are only true when you choose to believe them. They are something you choose many times unconsciously. Your beliefs can be changed by choosing empowering ones that will change your life. Your belief system is your rule book for your life. You use it to make decisions, create your reality, and view your world and your place in it. It is important to know that many beliefs you choose unconsciously. You accepted them from your parents or influential people without knowing that they were just someone else's beliefs and not necessarily right for you. Other beliefs were formed by how you experience people's reactions to your needs.

No matter how you form them, the majority were formed before you even began to develop your ability to reason. This all leads to your living by a set of rules that doesn't support you in what you are meant to be. You are unique and your rules and your beliefs must support that uniqueness, so you not only begin to understand that you are meant for more, but you also learn you have everything you need to live a life full of more.

A life full of more abundance, better health, more happiness, a life of high vibration, the life you are meant to live, and making the difference you are meant to make.

You are Universal Energy. You can create, manifest, and materialize any of the unlimited possibilities available to you in the Universe. When you choose the possibilities that are in alignment with you, with who you are and your mission on Earth, the more it comes easily.

In this now, Namaste.

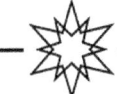

Michele's Musings

I cried when I listened to Vince's audio of this Active Connection. What was triggered? Perhaps I was familiar with the three major limiting beliefs more than I would have liked. For decades, I internalized the belief of being born flawed, along with an inherited sinful nature. I grew up in a large family with strong parents and siblings, all confident, succeeding, and well-liked by the community. Did feeling loved cross their minds, or were they just living day-to-day? I cannot speak for them, but I would not have perceived that there was more to life, or us, or that I was deserving of more. We were going through the motions of school, working on the farm, eating, and sleeping, all on autopilot, and it was not easy. Perceiving self-worth, feeling loved, being good enough, and feeling that we deserved and were meant for more might have made things a little easier. But that is not the way it was.

I am finding that the "more" referred to by the guides does not necessarily mean easy. It is said that we can and do choose our reality, whether we believe or realize it. Did I really choose my family before I was born? It is good and not-so-good news. Awareness of or awakening to how we attract whatever is/was/will be in our lives feels like a heavy responsibility. The good news is, yes, the possibilities of what our lives can look like are endless! The caveat, though, to my understanding, is our responsibility in raising our energetic vibration (how we feel) higher up the emotional scale (contentment, joy, happiness, empowerment, love, etc.) to where what we want is aligned with our current state. That is the sweet spot of attracting, being aligned with our energy, and a magnet for more—more than we ever expected or thought we deserved.

But this concept leaves many questions. When my body is in pain, I drop into the lower part of the emotional scale (despair, frustration, anger). I can choose to tell myself something different (change my thoughts) and transform my low energy into a higher emotional state. But what about young children with serious health challenges? How could they attract a potential lifetime of difficulties at a young age?

I am also curious if there are humans on Earth who grew up without these limiting beliefs or any beliefs that limited their perception of more. They would have had to be born in a bubble, not affected or influenced by any environment or other human. What would their lives look like? Or is conditioning just a part of the human condition, where we are born knowing, then having it replaced before the age of reason, as our environments and the people in them envelop us then gradually squeeze out our knowing of the larger truth of us? This begs the question then: Do generational factors play a role in beliefs we are born with? Eventually, we grow up and spend our lives bumping along, remembering here and there, some curiously wanting to figure it all out, some remaining comfortably on autopilot until death.

I attracted many "someones" into my life who mirrored the big three limiting beliefs. In early dating years I chose unhealthy relationships. The parenting style I experienced growing up emphasized succeeding with toughness and resiliency. In my part of the world, there was little energy or resources for coddling and nurturing. That, among other influences, fortified these beliefs as constant companions. The rules and stories built for me from others' beliefs became how I defined and maneuvered myself. I did not realize until later in life how disempowering beliefs left their mark on every area throughout my adulthood and, more importantly, that I chose them at some level, and I could change them and choose otherwise.

When I was young, "It's okay not to be more" paralleled with being humble and contrite, and the unwritten rule was not to draw attention, and God forbid, not to boast about your talents! The expectation was to never rock the boat. On one hand, play it small; but on the other, get out there and win, live up to our expectations because you should never be bad at school, sports, and church, *and* you must follow the rules. Reflecting success, hard work, and a virtuous and outward solid appearance was the common model for many I knew growing up in the sixties and seventies.

Another interesting belief is that I was duped by my parents, church, community, and teachers. The reality is they were not trying to trick me; they shared their best beliefs that other influential adults shared with them at a young age and so on throughout past generations. I felt like a victim even though their guiding and teaching was done with loving intentions. I became overly cautious, skeptical, and distrustful. It was me versus them. Thankfully, blame gently melts away as I gain understanding and compassion.

I made a significant decision to marry when I was too young and emotionally immature. It was made from the beliefs that I am not safe alone and that I needed to be taken care of and validated by another person, especially someone who would raise my perceived worth in the eyes of others. The beliefs resulted in a significant error of judgment and a union that did not last.

The guidance in the Active Connection that there is no such thing as mistakes or coincidences is challenging to understand. I bristle with that concept. So, my first marriage was not a mistake but a decision I made (unconsciously at the time) based on beliefs, insecurities, fears, etc., that I had about myself. It would mean that everything we experience is created by us, with us, for us, by what the guides refer to as our Higher Self, the nonphysical part of ourselves. And all for the bigger picture, the shift, as we raise our energetic frequency as a collective of humans on Earth and move into the new paradigm. I continue to work at understanding this, especially the *no-mistakes* part.

The guides explain how our beliefs are also based on how we experience people's reactions to our needs. When only positive emotions are supported, our needs are unmet, and we internalize the belief that we are not deserving, good enough, loved, or worthy. Something similar happens when emotions such as anger, sadness, frustration, etc., are suppressed in our youth and when only positive emotions are supported. As Bernadette Pleasant says, "When we bury emotions, we bury them alive." That inevitably becomes a bountiful harvest of problems as we grow into adulthood with unresolved emotions. We react in unhealthy, heightened ways, believing we are victims of the events and people in our lives. Imagine the ball in the pinball machine, never feeling in control of what happens to us, just getting emotionally pushed around. And even more interesting is that nothing happens *to* us; it all happens *because* of us, and our beliefs create all of it. When we are more consciously creating our beliefs in alignment with why we chose to be here, as the guides explained, we live a more purposeful and fulfilling life.

So, my understanding is that the soil is primed for subpersonalities at a vulnerable age, and these ego-self-caretakers proceed to protect our fragility with a constant barrage of stifling messages. The best part of this scenario, though, is that this rule book for life can be rewritten as we recognize the beliefs behind lower frequency, disempowering emotions and reactions. Recognizing them is half the battle, and the other half is knowing how to change them.

Do my current rules support my uniqueness? Do I understand I am meant for more abundance, better health, and to make a difference in the world? I hope so, even if it is just in my little corner. The possibilities are all for choosing if my vibration aligns with what I want. Then it is off to the races, right? It is easy when things are going well. If I am confronted or in a room where there is confrontation, my system becomes dysregulated. Nothing puts me into flight, freeze, or fawn mode more quickly. Fight response has never been within my reach.

An attendee at a recent small social gathering made ugly comments about our current environment of understanding and respect, where people categorize themselves on the list of gender identities. It was uncomfortable. Rather than calmly share my thoughts on inclusivity, respect, and acceptance, I listened, shocked and wide-eyed, and then changed the subject. I was thinking to myself, *If people different from us are not hurting or affecting our day-to-day existence, why is there anger toward them?* I do not understand hostile divisiveness, but the scenario showed clearly that I have work to do in regulating my nervous system, in responding, not reacting, and in raising the frequency of my energy and the environments that I am a part of, especially in low energetic frequency conversations.

Imagine looking at journals from years ago and reading all the same things that still manage to derail a good day or plummet a high frequency energy state. It is a little disheartening reading journal entries over several years describing the same struggles, the same things that hurt, frustrate, disappoint, and upset me. I did not know then how to change my underlying beliefs and that I could perceive things differently. I am making new rules based on empowering beliefs. I am more conscious as I move about my days, transforming my default energetic frequency to the highest possible and creating the *more* that I am meant for in this lifetime.

Vince and Mary's Reflections

The magic in this guidance is the message that we are all meant for more. Although it isn't specifically shared in this session, it has been shared many times in the past—much more. Not just more in one area of life either. They share that there is much more for us in every area of life. We don't know about you, but that excites us. We have heard too many people say, "Life doesn't get any better than this" or "That's as good as it gets." We all feel that there is more, but we are too willing to give up or worse, just take others' word for it.

Lack is a learned restriction, often driven by or at least influenced by beliefs. Many of our beliefs are accepted by society without question. It was pertinent and important for you to hear from guidance that they aren't real and that you get to choose your own. We build our own rulebook for life. Let's make it an empowering one, designed *for* you and *by* you!

There are many reasons why this particular piece of guidance might create emotion. As Michele shared, we are all too familiar with the three most common beliefs about humans. But we also have an innate knowing or understanding that we are meant for more. We are called to it. For some, this calling is constant. Others experience it from time to time. But we all have it. Guidance tells us not to ignore the calling or the emotions associated with it.

When Michele stated knowing that we attract our experiences into our lives is a big responsibility, she couldn't have been more right. The important part of this, in our opinion, is that it is our responsibility. When Vince first understood that concept, he was actually relieved. If he was the only one responsible for his life, no one else could be. That meant he couldn't be a victim. Don't get us wrong, that truly is a big paradigm shift, and it can be a very empowering one.

To address Michele's question about anyone growing up without limiting beliefs, we believe we all have them. But they aren't our curse. They are our motivators, protectors, and opportunities. But there comes a time to discover you have them and move beyond them. When they have outlived their usefulness, whatever that is, it is time to reframe them or choose new ones that support us. And yes, we all can do it.

Beliefs can be very generational. Beliefs are really nothing more than thoughts that we think over and over again. We attract into our lives proof that these thoughts are correct and then make our newfound belief a rule for our life. A collective belief comes from several people having these thoughts and sharing them with others. Soon, you see articles about the belief and documentaries. We start diagnosing or labeling people as this or that. Soon, an entire generation has been labeled. They have been told how their life is, where it isn't fair, and how an entire age group has been diminished or treated wrong. They begin to believe it more and more, attracting proof. And just like that, a whole new generation has a belief that limits them. Before long, all of society begins to accept the belief as the way it is, and a collective belief is formed.

We all have a life that we are meant to live, and this guidance points us in the right direction and gives us an understanding of how to get out of our own way.

Introspective Insights:

(Take a few minutes to journal or meditate on the following questions.)

1. Where have you been limited by the beliefs given to you by society?
2. What does "being meant for more" mean to you?
3. What beliefs have been holding you back and keeping you stuck?
4. What beliefs do you want to help you create the life you are meant to live?

Chaos Explained
(AC 23 Jan 24)

Source energy is constantly growing and expanding. In that growth and expansion, much chaos can and will be experienced as you move into the new paradigm of that expansion. The chaos is felt mostly by those who choose not to grow and expand with the whole in their earthly existence.

The Round Table, channeled by Vince Kramer

Why is there so much chaos as we are shifting into the new paradigm?

Yes, we would be honored to help you understand this. You have heard us explain that you are all creators of your reality and that there is movement toward and into the new paradigm. Everything is created from the energy of the Universe. Creation for each of you starts with your thoughts. As soon as you have a thought, you have created.

It is identifying, and if you will, choosing one of the unlimited possibilities available to you in the Universe. If you continue to think about it, you turn the possibility into a probability. You also start to bring your feelings into the creation process. The language of the Universe is electromagnetic. Your thoughts are energy, thus electromagnetic. Your feelings are energy, thus electromagnetic. Everything is electromagnetic. Thoughts are mostly electric, and feelings are mostly magnetic. As you continue to hold what you want and what you want to create in your thoughts and your feelings of having it aligned with your thoughts, you become energetically aligned with what you want, and you begin to manifest your creation into your life. As long as you continue to hold what you want in your thoughts and if you don't hold the thoughts of not having it energetically, the energy of what you want unfolds into the materialization of what you want.

So basically, the creation process of creating, manifesting, and materializing causes the Universal Energy to UNFOLD in what you have kept your thoughts on and your feelings aligned with. The opposite happens when there is something you no longer want or that you want to transform.

We prefer for you to transform and not change. We can share more about that at another time. The energy enfolds, ENFOLDS from materialized back into Universal Energy to be used again to create. What is happening as you move into the new paradigm is the old way of being is enfolding, and the new way of being is *un*folding. This creates chaos and uneasiness. It mixes things up, as you will.

It causes resistance in some. It causes excitement in some. It forces the status quo to no longer be acceptable, and this causes the energy to be turbulent as you move into the unknown. This is what you are observing or participating in when you ask about the chaos as you move into the new paradigm. This is what's causing what seems to be more separation. This is what's causing the split in politics, neighborhoods, and countries. It is even causing splits in families. You are experiencing the energy enfolding from the old and being replaced, unfolding with the energy of the new, into this new paradigm, of which we speak into the *we consciousness.*

This is all explained in your science that you call quantum physics or quantum mechanics. It is important for you to know that this science can help you understand how you as energy are the creator of your life and how you affect others and they affect you, because you and us are all one energy.

In this now, Namaste.

Michele's Musings

I have had a love-hate relationship with the Law of Attraction. The guide's explanation of how our thoughts create our reality sounded like that concept. I was one of the millions who watched *The Secret* years ago, and although skeptical, a part of me considered *What if?* And what if the science behind it (that I never understood a word of at the time) was sound? On the other hand, it frustrated me because what if I did what I was supposed to do to create what I wanted, and it still did not happen? It would mean I got it wrong or, worse, that something *else* was wrong with me or I was undeserving. But it was around this time that I no longer perceived myself as religious, so the window was nudged open a crack, enough to consider a way of seeing the world that was safely distanced from previously held religious beliefs.

An unfortunate incident took me further into the Law of Attraction and the thoughts-create-our-reality notion. I had finished writing a book about coming out of religion, happily accepting that there is no hell, that we live then we die, and that there is no rhyme or reason to any of our random existence. I had been basking in the freedom of that perspective. Then it happened. Some refer to this as a *wake-up call*. It was not instant, but it was a profound start to getting the ball rolling. Considering my usual slow roll, it took the impact of the incident and all the nuances that flowed from it for me to consider the connection between our thoughts and feelings and the creation process, how we electromagnetically attract what our energy is aligned with.

But first, a limiting belief... I never had a therapist because therapists are for people who are not equipped or strong enough to handle the expected stressors of life. That was my belief until it wasn't.

It started shortly after my Lhasa apso was attacked by a rottweiler. I could not fall asleep. The image of the rottweiler kept flashing in my mind, slamming my small dog's limp body in the dirt like a wet mop. Her jaws remained clenched on Cooper's little neck, refusing to let go despite my fist pounding on her thick back. There seemed to be nothing that I could do but witness her determined will to kill my six-year-old Lhasa apso.

I was screaming. I could taste blood in my mouth. She would not stop. It seemed to last longer, but it was probably less than a minute. When she loosened her grip enough for me to grab Cooper up into my arms, I ran toward my house; she was growling, chasing us, and biting at my legs. I saw another neighbor running toward my yard from his acreage, responding to my screams. The rottweiler had turned back toward her property.

The neighbor drove us to the city to the veterinary clinic. I was sobbing, and Cooper and I were shaking uncontrollably. I had blood on my hands, and I could see blood on Cooper's neck. I was not ready to say goodbye to my beloved pet. My husband met me in the city, and we drove around and waited for the call. I was exhausted from crying. Two hours later, the veterinarian called us back to the clinic. Cooper had several tears and puncture wounds, and time would tell if he would survive.

Fast forward a few weeks, and Cooper healed, but I did not. It was my fault. I had put him in harm's way. Panicked, I would wake up during the night with nightmares, reliving the incident. What the hell? We both survived! I did not understand this overreaction. I sought help begrudgingly. Not only did I not protect my little dog, but I also failed to get through the ordeal. Maybe just a few quick sessions and I could return to much-needed, normal sleep. I wanted to be able to just move on.

The therapist was kind and had a welcomed sense of humor. I shared that I needed some quick commonsense tools to slide through this unsettling blip in my usually contented existence. I also emphasized the "commonsense" part. I did not want any other-worldly-based help. I did not need healing in a spiritual or God sense. I had scanned her therapy room earlier for crosses, pictures of Jesus, or his mom.

I enjoyed the first session and left with some practical ways to deal with intense sleep interruptions. Soon, I returned to my usual slumber. Within every session I found new insights into life and how to best maneuver. The therapeutic process was interesting and helpful.

I saw her again when challenges arose. During one session, she asked if I had ever heard of Jerry and Esther Hicks. I searched my mind… I vaguely remembered hearing these names as hosts of a hyper-religious late-night radio show. I was relieved to find that it was not them, but I thought, *Yeesh! I like you; please do not do something weird and mess up our therapeutic relationship!*

With an eye roll, I checked them out. They did not call it channeling, but it was my first serious consideration of connecting with nonphysical energy and as explained in this Active Connection, we create our reality. Also, our thoughts are powerful in whatever we attract into our lives. It was not just "Abracadabra!" where we snapped our fingers, and a new car landed magically in the driveway. There is a process and a responsibility to manage our energetic frequency. It is also not positive thinking, which feels phony and minimizes our complex but natural emotional processes.

Realizing and integrating what we create with our thoughts is the movement toward the new paradigm, where we understand that everything is energy. We draw to ourselves whatever our energy is aligned with. We choose day-to-day what the frequency of our energy is. And no, it is not a pie-in-the-sky utopia because we are human, and we maneuver along the spectrum of frequencies from low experiences to high. But, regardless of what unfolds in our day-to-day living, we control our thoughts and emotions, and we decide how we deal or not, what we want and do not want, and under-standing how we think about everything affects how we feel. This is a shift in mainstream thinking, especially the idea that we are victims and that things happen *to* us rather than by us and for us. With this paradigm shift, there is chaos. I feel it. There are days I feel like I am going completely against the grain, that I am just wrong again. And then, how far down the rabbit hole will I allow myself to go?

I tested the authenticity of Esther Hicks (for longer than I care to admit), as she was connecting with the energy of a group referred to as Abraham. I wanted to catch her saying "I" instead of "we." Esther never slipped! Not once! This was several years ago, and it ended up being my gateway drug to unleashing the curiosities that lay dormant at the end of a first book I wrote. I have come across few "commonsense channelers" as authentic and aligned as Esther Hicks until recently. My experience with what Vince does when he connects is all that, including being so specific in how we maneuver in our human existence. The information is pragmatic, useful, relevant, and aligned with what I am currently learning, growing, and integrating. It resonates at a much deeper but realistic level.

So, had I co-created the whole horrible ordeal with Cooper? Was it to meet a therapist, to receive a palatable invitation to discover further the Law of Attraction? And then to trust the guidance of Abraham through Esther Hicks, which would open me further to attract the teachings of Vince and Mary and The Round Table and all the teachings unfolding through this creative process?

With nonjudgment, I observe people who are not curious or do not want to know their purpose in life or to seek answers to the bigger questions. I am not one of them, although I sometimes envy the indifference. As I am learning more about the new paradigm, I cannot go back to most of my days spent in an unconscious state, on autopilot. My sense of responsibility with this life and my desire to squeeze out every last drop of deserved excitement, adventure, enjoyment, and love that my time will allow keeps me hooked on thinking, growing, feeling, and learning. And that does not make me better or more enlightened than anyone else. It provides a spot on the map, gauging where I am and acknowledging that we are all in different places.

Sometimes, I feel chaos inside, like I need a bit of a wheel alignment and sometimes a bumper-to-bumper overhaul. The inner chaos, or the enfolding as the guides describe in the Active Connection, is unsettling; I feel like the bottom is dropping out from under my feet. Letting go of the need for certainty about the future especially and a deep inner need to feel safe despite the uncertainty surrounding the shift into the new paradigm is sometimes unnerving. At the same time, I am witnessing myself moving into experiencing my personal energy expanding and unfolding. I am choosing to take a leap and trust the inner transformation. Then again, the feeling of chaos surfaces with the critical, fearful voice of my psyche, my subpersonalities that are forever loyal, the guardians of the gate, keeping me cautiously aware as I move forward despite what others will think of me.

Then I feel what is going on outside of me as the energetic frequency of the Universe continues to expand. Naturally, and uncomfortably, there is some uneasiness with movement toward the new paradigm because it is new and different from the old paradigm. And, if I am understanding it correctly, the expanded energy frequency of the new paradigm continues to expand with or without a collective belief in it or conscious understanding of it. It just is. We can choose to jump on or not. With the new paradigm we raise our energetic vibration and look forward to enjoying an even more expanded state of higher energy frequencies of community, love, empowerment, happiness, contentment, and joy.

Vince and Mary's Reflections

We all need to embody the process of creation through thoughts and feelings. If we understand this process, there will be no doubt why we have created what we have up to now. And… there should be no doubt in how we can create what we want in the future. Understanding the process really gives us all the responsibility for our lives. For some, that might be uncomfortable.

The concepts of unfolding and enfolding can be easily explained. Basically, there is one energy. That energy makes up everything. When that energy is used to manifest and materialize something on our Earth, we can say the energy was unfolded into the physical object we created. When the object is no longer needed or wanted, it will return to the Universal Energy it was created from. This process is called enfolding. Once again, this is a very basic explanation that is more complex. But you understand the concept.

It makes sense that this unfolding and enfolding creates disruption or chaos. This certainly explains the craziness we are experiencing in our world in this transformation from "I" to "we" consciousness. It gives hope, knowing that if we hold our vibration, we can limit the effects of chaos, if not eliminate it.

We tend to want the world we live in to be black and white, right or wrong. The Universe and, in turn, our Earth isn't black and white. In fact, it is every color all the time. It is a hard concept to accept because of everything we have been taught and our collective beliefs. We play the lead role in our lives and how we create them. We live in a world where everything just "is." I'm sure we will cover that concept in a future book. It is the black-and-white ways that left Michele feeling as she describes above.

Everything happens for a reason, no mistakes or coincidences. Like Michele, we might not want to or even be able to see the creation or the gift in it. The incident with Michele's dog, Cooper, started her on a path of awakening and seeing life in a new way. Were her thoughts and feelings aligned with waking up and seeing a new way? Our guess is they were.

> **Introspective Insights:**
> (Take a few minutes to journal or meditate on the following questions.)
> 1. Can you see where your thoughts and feelings have created your life?
> 2. How can you become empowered with the new understanding of this Active Connection?
> 3. Can you find in the life circumstances that you have created where you have been given a gift of insight?
> 4. Where are you looking at the world from a black-and-white vantage point and staying stuck?

Trust
(AC 15 Jan 24)

There is all the knowledge of the Universe available if you are just willing to ask the questions. You also must be willing to uncover your answers to the questions you ask. When you resist either asking or uncovering, you are the obstacle to the life you are meant to live and to making the difference you are meant to make.

The Round Table, channeled by Vince Kramer

Recently, we talked about getting and receiving guidance. We have so much resistance to believing we are getting guidance. Can you address why there is this resistance?

> Yes, certainly. Most, if not all, of an individual's resistance comes from beliefs, self-judgment, or fear of being wrong. We will expand on each. Beliefs have much to do with receiving and, just as important, accepting guidance.
>
> You all have personal beliefs about your ability to receive guidance. First, is it possible? Are you worthy? There are so many voices in your head. How will you know? There are more doubts or questions than people asking. Many beliefs formed around religion or against religion can play a big part in the belief.

You can actually talk to guides, God, Source, etc. You have been told throughout your years on your planet that these vibrations or frequencies are outside of you, better than you. You've been taught that you are crazy to believe that you are hearing voices or getting information. You have even been told that it is the devil trying to trick you. All of this deters you from trusting that you are actually tapping into this universal knowledge available to you.

Throughout the years, you have heard people declared crazy or ridiculed because they were talking to angels or the dead. Parents have told children they were wrong because they told their parents they were visited by or talked to the angels. These things that we have shared all lead to beliefs that getting your guidance in this way is wrong or means you are mentally unstable. This belief shuts you down or, at the very least, deters you from allowing this information to come through to you. And, if it does come through, it prevents you from acknowledging it.

Another reason for resistance or lack of trust is self-judgment. Many have been taught that they are separate from this energy. This leads to believing the guides or angels being more important or higher in status than you. These people doubt if they deserve to get this connection. They say things like, Who am I to talk to God or source? And who am I to get answers to my prayers?

This self-judgment leads to thinking that the answers that do come through are made up or that you are just getting your own answers from your mind. You think it is not coming from the highest frequencies.

First, notice in the answers that you receive where there are things that you never would say or maybe don't even believe. This will help you move beyond the concern that you are making it up. Also, ask from guidance for some type of proof that you are connecting with the higher frequencies. You can and will get this proof if you allow it.

Last, let us discuss fear. Many are afraid even to attempt to connect with and receive guidance because they are afraid they won't be able to, and subconsciously, they prove to themselves that they are unworthy or that there is truly something wrong with them. This fear is a big enough deterrent that they don't want to even try, and they come up with many justifications not to.

Others are afraid they will connect with evil energies, energies that will give them bad advice or try to corrupt them. Know that there are only high and low vibrations, not good and evil vibrations.

If you move forward with this understanding and with the highest intentions, the experiences you will have will only be from the highest vibrations. The vibration you hold is the vibration you attract. The highest vibrations of your energy stream are waiting to guide you and assist you in being all you are meant to be, all that you want to be. They want to help you trust and believe. They want you to be all that you can be.

It was your choice to come to the Earth and to make this difference. Know that the higher vibrations are all in alignment with supporting that choice, guiding you on the journey you chose, and providing you greater access to all knowledge and understanding. Trust us and believe in you.

In this now, Namaste.

Michele's Musings

One of my most ingrained beliefs about guidance is that it comes only from outside of me, and normally only after due diligence do I discern if the source is credible. The underlying fear I have realized is of being wrong again, as I was with past belief systems.

As I read this Active Connection, I recalled that over the years, my grandmother has been gently revealing her nonphysical energy as guidance. Through this short story, I share a connection that continues beyond our perception of end of life.

It was spring, 1981. Our graduating class of twenty-five students had practiced the song for months, "This Will Be Our Last Song Together," Nana Mouskouri's rendition. My dress was recycled from when I was a junior bridesmaid at a family wedding. It was full-length, cream-colored, and made of a flowing and softly pleated material. My aunt made changes by adding pretty, silk, brown ribbons to it. I loved it. And it was free. Regrettably, I had gotten a new hairstyle in preparation for the big day. It was awful! Too short for my face, unfortunately a style that was not flattering at all. But I was graduating, ready for the next chapter, and other than my first trainer bra at fourteen, the most significant transition in my young life.

My grandmother was very excited about the occasion and showed me her new dress weeks in advance. I had spent much time with her during my high school years. She was loving and nurturing and treated me like I was special and that I could do no wrong. I often stayed out significantly past my curfew on school nights, and when my mom asked the time I had arrived home the previous night, my grandma just shrugged her shoulders to say that she was not sure. She was protective and provided unconditional support and unforgettable hugs that I soaked up happily. I felt safe with her. Although she has been gone for decades, I am forever grateful for the many sacred secrets we hold.

During the graduation ceremony, just as my name was announced as the recipient of the RCMP (Royal Canadian Mounted Police) Student of the Year Award for all-around outstanding student, my grandmother fainted! She loved me; she was overwhelmed, and the excitement had gotten the best of her. She recovered shortly after and left the physical a few years later. I was shocked about the award, as I was not the most popular, and I was a farm girl with hand-me-down clothes from cousins and family friends. I wasn't special. I was the country mouse, insecure to the core, wearing a recycled dress and sporting a horrible haircut!

My memories of my grandmother remind me of our connection with nonphysical energy, even though I did not understand it conceptually during the times over the years when I had felt her guidance from the nonphysical realm. Trusting it as a constant source of guidance and support was challenging, even as she connected with my dreams and shared love and support. I tend to find it easier still to consider trusting her nonphysical guidance more than the angels and masters, perhaps because of our connection during her physical life. Interestingly, though, I have more trust in the outside guidance of Vince's Active Connections and also the personal and deeply revealing sessions with The Round Table.

The guidance in this Active Connection shares some of the reasons for resistance to trusting it. I have perceived what comes from outside of me as more real than my own guidance, especially as others connect with the big guns: the Archangels, the power couple Jeshua and Miriam of Magdala (a.k.a. Jesus and Mary Magdalene), the powerful goddesses, the lovely lineage of the divine feminine (Isis, Yeshua's grandma Anna, Mother Mary, etc.), and a whole host of Ascended Masters. What if the guidance, all of it, actually comes from *inside* of us, as we connect with and are part of all of the energies?

Still today, adults will make children wrong for believing in invisible friends or spirit guides. It does not take long for children to begin to doubt themselves and to no longer trust their little, inner, nonphysical voices.

I have strived to be perceived as credible, logical, sane, not gullible, and more of a critical thinker. When I left religion, it was through years of soul searching, research, the painstaking writing of a book, a written testimony of sorts, and eventually realizing my beliefs had evolved significantly. I am grateful, since then, that fear-based beliefs continue to dissolve, but there exists a fear that if I ask for guidance and it does not come, then I did something wrong or was just not deserving. I would meditate and ask please, please, please help me with this or that. I would plead, "Do I feel you?" "Do I hear you?" "Please show me you are here, that I am not talking to empty space!" Still nothing. Training in the Akashic Records felt closer to feeling something, but there was still too much doubt.

It was not until Take a Quantum Leap exercises with Active Connection that I felt like I was connecting and receiving guidance and that it was from inside of me. I was asking questions and getting answers. The trust ebbed and flowed throughout the course, and the experiences reminded me of intuitive writing practices from the past, where I would quiet my mind to tune in. But, with time, after the course, as often happens, the fruits of learning and experiencing faded, gradually replaced with living normal day-to-day life, unplugged, mostly on autopilot. The Active Connections and my noticing and trusting the guidance dwindled.

My focus recently shifted while immersed in the Quantum Circle program with Vince and Mary. The CREATE Model eased me back to my inner self and toward understanding the reasons behind not trusting the guidance, beginning to trust again, and the daily co-creating occurring as I become more conscious of maneuvering with intention and purpose.

And now to this writing project where idea bubbles rise into my head as I do the laundry, empty the dishwasher, and tell stories of potentially relatable experiences relevant to the various Active Connections. I wake up with inspired thoughts as I put in my order every night with an intent to be conscious of specific guidance the following day. These are still early days of trusting for me.

I have been a simmering slow cooker, so to speak, in this whole waking-up process. My skepticism, a stubborn beast and a sturdy soldier of protection, my voices of numerous subpersonalities alive and well, and my heart overruling with gentle nudges like, *It is okay to trust, to open up, to accept all parts of you, to be vulnerable and connect with others. It is okay to ask, to trust the answers, to discover self-acceptance, compassion, and feeling safe, always from inside yourself.*

Vince and Mary's Reflections

When we talk about sabotage, not moving forward, or being stuck, beliefs are mentioned. Our belief system is a big part of our operating system, better known as our personality. Beliefs are the foundation of our reality. It also makes sense that the subject of tapping in or receiving guidance is affected by our belief system. It is mentioned several times in this book that beliefs aren't real and that the willingness to change them will empower us. But it is the beliefs of others or the fear of what they will think about us that holds us back. We can't blame others for their beliefs if they don't know they can change them. But we can choose to take that understanding and make our experience with guidance even more supportive by changing our own beliefs. Receiving this guidance doesn't show that you are crazy; it isn't the devil, and it certainly doesn't mean you are wrong or unstable in your thinking.

Although self-judgment comes from our beliefs, it is important that we talk about it separately from them. When it comes to judging our worthiness, it seems many don't believe they are worthy or good enough to receive guidance. Who are we to tap into the higher vibrations? We judge ourselves much harsher than we judge others, believing we aren't special and deserve little. The opposite is true. We must learn to see ourselves for who we truly are.

Michele is not alone in being able to trust the guidance through others more than when she receives it herself. It illustrates the self-judgment we just talked about. It is also easier to accept guidance from someone we are very familiar with, plus the vibration is closer to our own. The higher the vibration, the more complex the message. This results in not trusting the message.

Michele is an example of learning to trust and surrender. The more she does, the freer the flow of guidance. The freer the flow of guidance, the more she understands it and trusts it.

> **Introspective Insights:**
> (Take a few minutes to journal or meditate on the following questions.)
> 1. Where have you shut yourself off from receiving guidance?
> 2. When have you judged yourself as being not worthy or good enough?
> 3. What did you learn from others about guidance, and how did it stifle you?
> 4. Where do you doubt your knowingness and listen to others over yourself?

Separateness
(AC 20 Jan 24)

There is only one energy. You are all a part of this energy, and the entirety of this energy is you. There is no you and me. There is no yours or mine. You are all everything, and you must love every part of you unconditionally to support the collective in moving fully into we consciousness.

The Round Table, channeled by Vince Kramer

You have previously shared about duality and separateness. We have seen so much of it worldwide and in our country in the last few years. Can you share why we are seeing so much of it?

> As we have shared with you in the past, your planet is moving into a new paradigm, a new way of thinking and being. Where there is change or transformation afoot, there is resistance for those on your Earth who have awakened or are awakening to this new way of being, who will be aware of not just the movement to this new paradigm but also of the growing resistance to it.
>
> Also, without even knowing it, there will be many who will cling to the old because they will feel the energetic movement toward the new.

What are we sharing here? We are sharing that there is definitely evidence of more separation in the world in the resistance. But as you and many awaken to more of who you truly are, you'll see it more in the world.

There are many places where you can see the old ways around you. One of the biggest is in politics. It is one side against the other with very little compromise or agreement between them. It is one way or my way. It isn't our way. This separation has gone much deeper with personal attacks and accusations.

Many of these politicians worry about losing their power in a new or different way that they feel is coming. They use the fears of those they represent. They use it to manipulate or scare people. They use their own truths and sometimes outright lies to stoke the fears. They amplify the fears creating support for the duality and separateness that is being desperately held onto to maintain the power.

They are holding on to this power because they know no other way and believe in what we have shared. At this moment, the world you live in is based on either/or.

For those of you who see the separation, you can change it. Most importantly, know that what you experience on the outside is nothing more than a mirror for you. For those who are experiencing the separation, no matter how you are experiencing it, you must know that by observing it in the world and being triggered by it, you are being shown the separateness in you.

Just like everything that is experienced in the collective energy, the only way you can help shift the collective energy is to shift the energy or, more correctly, transform the energy in you. It is about seeing and accepting all parts of you. It is about not judging any part of you, seeing it as good or bad, right or wrong, or acceptable or unacceptable. The growth and expansion you will be experiencing can and will be an energetic force that will raise the vibration of the collective.

You will be the example for others to find the separation in them. As you move into the higher vibration, you will see the separation for what it is, the precursor of the new paradigm, the resistance to oneness, and the uncertainty it might bring. You can and must hold the higher vibration in your support and the support of the collective in moving into the higher vibrations of the new paradigm. Each person who moves forward brings the new paradigm closer and moves beyond the separation you see and experience.

In this now, Namaste.

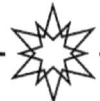

Michele's Musings

I heard it again recently: "Forget what you learned up until now, and remember what you knew before you started forgetting." I was on a coaching call with Vince when it landed. Six decades is a lot of learning to forget! My old way of thinking was that we are separate, competing, us against them, even in my closest relationships.

As I was reading this Active Connection and sort of feeling into the concept of separateness rather than thinking about times when I felt separate, I remembered a specific time when the feeling of separateness was completely absent. Now that my understanding and awareness have increased, I have been conscious of oneness more often, but through this incident, I experienced it beyond my five senses.

It happened a few years ago. The summer storm was one of the worst I had seen. Trees were uprooted, roofs torn off in the city. Our acreage was not damaged other than things strewn around the yard and small branches broken. It was the day after, and my husband was helping our son's neighbor in the city cut a large branch that had broken partly off a huge tree. He was on a ladder with a chainsaw just trying to get a quick neighborly job done, and as the chainsaw chewed through enough of the branch, the weight of it caused it to twist and swing down, sweeping the lower part of the ladder out from under him. The ladder was broken, and so was his pelvis. He did not know it then, as he continued helping the neighbor, driving his truck for one last trip to haul the debris away and then home to our place. I helped him get into the house and onto the bed. He was in so much pain. I finally convinced him he needed an ambulance. He had a bruised head, three pelvic fractures, and a torn tendon in his shoulder.

A brief backstory: I am not a natural caretaker AT ALL! I admire people who are equipped with such a selfless gene. I care deeply about people but never feel compelled or a desire to care for them, especially physically. In fact, my husband had mentioned a few times over the years that he was quite sure if something ever happened to him that I would not stick around. That sounds horrible, as I share it, but I married someone as strong as a horse, protective to the death, a military and penitentiary guy who takes care of many things that I do not care about or want to manage. I joke that he enjoys this role, and I would not want to take that joy away from him. He enjoys cooking, grocery shopping, and building, and true to his reputation, he can and does fix anything. He makes day-to-day life very comfortable for us. So, yes, I do not want to say I need him, but I do prefer to have him remain healthy and able-bodied. And again, how privileged this sounds, yes, I may have been spoiled rotten.

He was bedridden, with the risk of the fractures displacing and, according to the surgeon, potentially requiring surgery and a body cast for several months. Mostly, I was grateful that he did not die, and then I was terrified that if we were not cautious, the fractured bones would be displaced. I could never take care of the land on my own. I had retired two months earlier, so the timing was convenient for me to step up, but this was out of my comfort zone.

I would say that it was the most vulnerable I had seen him over our thirty-plus years together. I cried for him, and I cried for me, and not just because I had to take care of things myself during this time; his suffering was my suffering. I could not fix him; surrendering to time was my only option. I remember sitting on the bathroom floor during one of the early days, drying him off after the shower. He was in such intense pain. I felt an unfamiliar wave of compassion well up in my heart. It expanded with so much love it overwhelmed me. Two human beings connected, with no hint of separateness in my cells. There was a remembering that surfaced, a knowing on a visceral level. This was probably a micro glimpse of the oneness the guides refer to in the Active Connection.

They explain that the separation we see in the world is a mirror of our separateness. A serious accident showed me something important about human connection and deep love for another. It directed me to my heart and revealed its capacity. It showed me parts of myself that I did not accept and, at times, still struggle to accept. Was my default position with my husband selfish and entitled? Am I expecting too much from another human being, especially my lack of feeling safe? I am learning the importance of finding that inside, but it is not easy when the foundation of an inner feeling of safety is void from formative years. The guides emphasize not judging any part of us as good or bad, right or wrong, acceptable or unacceptable. That is a mission I am currently on, as I am working through the elements of the CREATE Model in Mary and Vince's Quantum Circle program.

I look forward to less judgment of myself, but will it ever be complete acceptance? Is that possible? Is that the higher vibration that will shift us away from the separateness I see in myself and the world? The resistance is palpable, but the shift is the hope of the new paradigm; the more we shift our individual frequency, the more we will shift the energetic frequency of the collective. Imagine humanity spending more and more time in their thoughts and day-to-day interactions in the higher emotional states of joy, appreciation, empowerment, freedom, and love. Yes, even in our politics and our families.

Vince and Mary's Reflections

We find it important to emphasize that much of the separateness we are experiencing is a result of moving into a new way, a way where we are there for each other and support each other in living the lives we are meant to live. It is so difficult to experience the evidence of the contrary through our five senses. Is this truly a necessary experience to get from where we are to where we have chosen to be at a higher, more expanded level?

It is challenging for us to accept that what we see on the outside is a mirror of who we are on the inside. And then, to take it even further, we can transform ourselves, and that will help transform the outside. Can you believe you are that powerful? Are you willing to accept that responsibility? We are meant to be the example of how it can be. You are reading this right now, which means you chose to be a major part of this transition.

When Michele shares that she experienced great connectedness with her husband, that is also a mirror to her of what it would be like to experience that same type of connectedness on the inside. The world around us and everything and anyone we attract into our lives is showing us something about ourselves. It is so beneficial to grasp that concept. Our work is an inside job. When we find oneness on the inside, it will be reflected by the outside.

The answers to Michele's questions in her last paragraph are all yes. We get to choose to live in those higher vibrations.

Introspective Insights:

(Take a few minutes to journal or meditate on the following questions.)

1. Where have you experienced a feeling of oneness with another person or a group of people?
2. When have you fostered separateness in your life, and how did it feel?
3. When do you judge parts of yourself or your actions?
4. How would life be different if you learned to love every part of yourself?

Higher Self
(AC 26 Jan 24)

You are a multidimensional being who chose the earthly experience to expand Universal Energy. Your existence is not a mistake or coincidence. You are a powerful creator living a life designed and blueprinted to support all that is and all that will ever be.

The Round Table, channeled by Vince Kramer

Who is or what is the Higher Self?

> In earlier times with you, we have used many terms for the same thing. We have talked about the nonphysical part of you, the soul, the higher vibration of you, and the Higher Self. All of these terms are the same thing.
>
> You are a stream or a strand of Universal Energy. The one true energy. This energy is called many things, mostly so each human can accept it or talk about it in their own way. There are twelve main strands of energy. Each of you chose to represent one of those main strands or a combination of these main strands. There are thousands of these combinations represented on your planet. Each strand or combination stretches from the highest possible

vibration of the strand or combination to the lowest of its vibrations, which are experienced in the third and fourth dimensions.

For ease of discussion, we will use the words *energy stream* to represent the strand or strands you each have chosen to represent. As we were saying, if you look at it from a linear perspective, one end of the stream is the highest vibration, that of the Universe or Source Energy, and your end of the whole stream represents the lowest frequency or vibration.

Let us talk about your end of the stream now. In your decision to come to your Earth, there was a need for part of the stream that you would call "you" to become physical. This part of you is the matter part of the stream, the flesh and bone part. It is what you and we call the human being part. This human part of you was required to forget all that you knew when you made the choice to live in the third and fourth dimensions. The majority of the energy stream that you vibrationally represent is nonphysical.

It is what we are talking about when we say the nonphysical or the Higher Self. We reference it as the Higher Self because it is the part you haven't forgotten. It knows and remembers why you chose this earthly experience and is responsible, if you will, for creating and co-creating every circumstance and experience in your 3D life to help you fully live the life you chose to live on Earth and make the difference as part of the whole that is your chosen mission. The combination of all the missions of each energy stream leads to the wholeness of the Universe experiencing itself and expanding itself into a higher vibration. This is much for you to consider.

In this now, Namaste.

Michele's Musings

I am only beginning to understand the concept of the Higher Self. One would think that after numerous courses, this concept would be fully integrated. Not so. Something happens to me, and maybe it is the overuse of the term *Higher Power* that is off-putting. Higher

Power is something *up there*, bigger than us, outside of us, fixing us, an implication that fixing is needed from something out of reach and more powerful than us. That was a belief I had, and as I am learning, no beliefs are real because beliefs can change. For someone who clings to wanting certainty, that is not easily integrated.

What I have been understanding recently is that my Higher Self is not what people refer to as Higher Power. First, for the Higher Self, it is not "higher," implying higher than me or that there is a hierarchy. It is the higher frequency part of me; it *is* me. During meditation, I perceive it not above my head but in my body, more specifically, my heart, which helps me feel like I am connecting. I have been practicing using Active Connection to tune into that deeper part of me that existed before this physical life. I understand it to be the aware and always remembering part of me. It seems like the orchestra conductor, a manager of sorts, having access to the bigger picture and working in my best interest as I get stuck in the mud, regularly. That sounds like the soul, and my understanding of the soul is also the nonphysical part of me that never ends. It is similar to the Higher Self, and it is my personal history as non-physical energy.

The guidance in this Active Connection clarifies things further. My Higher Self creates and co-creates every circumstance and experience in my 3D life. *EVERY* circumstance and experience? Wow! One comes to mind. I was turning sixty. I like to say a young sixty because there is no way I felt as old as I expected sixty to feel. It seems not so long ago that I turned fifty. Now, I look in the mirror and see clear evidence of aging. (I blame whoever came up with magnifying mirrors!) Not long ago, I realized this was resistance to aging. But resisting does no good at all; it only speeds up the aging process and causes more wrinkles! The clock never stops. My mortality stares me in the face every morning, igniting the slippery slope to disappointment and self-loathing, and voila! my energetic frequency is in the dumper. And the day has not started.

So, yes, I was scheduled to turn sixty last year. Knowing how much I dislike surprises, my daughter called one day and told me what was being planned: a small gathering of just immediate family, her being local, my sons traveling from four and six hours away, makeup and hair in the morning, family pictures and dinner, then glow bowling in the evening. How fun!! I was thrilled that they would go through the trouble for my birthday! My daughter decorated her home, and everyone arrived there the day before. I was giddy for days leading up to the celebration, excited my family would all be together and have a day of fun!

The day before the celebration, my husband started feeling sick. He declined quickly and stayed in bed, hoping to feel better for the next day. He got worse, then tested positive for COVID-19. My throat was already hurting, so I expected that I was infected as well. I never did test positive, but he ended up very sick for the following three weeks. I could not imagine my family being sick as a result of celebrating my birthday, so my husband and I chose to stay away.

My Higher Self decided for some greater reason or reasons that I would miss the rare occasion to be with all my family, celebrating me on that day, and the following few days. While they were traveling from event to event, they stopped on the street in front of our home. My husband got out of bed to wave at them from the deck balcony as they dropped off food on our front porch. We tried keeping it light and teased that he looked like the pope on Easter Sunday, waving down at the people in St. Peter's Square. I spoke to my granddaughters, being playful from my side of the fence. One of them was afraid and asked her mom to take her back to the car. My heart broke. There they all were, and I could not hug anyone or get physically close.

Yes, I am aware this was definitely not the extent of trauma many experienced during the pandemic, but I continued to cry for three days. I was grateful to them all for coming, especially when we are usually together only on rare occasions such as funerals or weddings. It meant so much to me because I know how hard it is to plan these things and have everyone attend.

So, Higher Self, how did we co-create that? What was the gift, as they say? As time passed, I had some ideas; none felt better than what the get-together would have been. It warmed my heart that the effort was made to celebrate my sixtieth, and I will always be grateful to them for that. I was also happy that they enjoyed their day together, and their efforts resulted in my feeling loved… maybe that was the gift.

I understand my energy strands are perceived as colors and that these nonphysical streams are named by us, which sort of personifies energy for our physical brains. We apply familiar or comfortable names to the strands. So, as mentioned in another chapter, I have three energy streams, and the colors are turquoise, pink, and orange. When I looked up what color is associated with the Archangels, I found Haniel, the energy of intuition, joy, and creativity; Chamuel, peaceful relationships, love of self and others, laughter, and child-like playfulness; and Uriel, the energy of wisdom, creativity, and positivity. I loved those! Of course I resonated!

They are me, and they are my energy streams. The guides in the Active Connection explain that the nonphysical is at the high end of the energy stream, and our 3D physical selves are at the lower frequency end. And the high frequency part makes up the majority of our selves, which is all connected to everyone's nonphysical selves on Earth. All of it, all of us are part of *the* energy, the only existing energy source.

According to the guides, the Higher Self helps us see magnificent opportunities, to be more, to develop our gifts and talents, and to see how magnificent we are. It is the higher vibrational part of me, and I am getting to know it, which sounds strange because it is like saying I am just getting to know my arm. Whether I believe my Higher Self is there or not, it never leaves me. It *is* me.

Vince and Mary's Reflections

How can anyone not be excited about this guidance? It explains so much and answers a lot of questions. First, it illustrates that there is only oneness. There is no separation. We are all a stream or a strand of the same energy. Each of us has multiple dimensions. The nonphysical part of us doesn't forget and constantly creates circumstances and situations for us to move into our highest vibrations.

No matter what you call that nonphysical part of us, it is our connection from the physical to the nonphysical. It is our connection from the lower vibrations to the highest vibrations.

Michele is not alone in being challenged with the term *Higher Power*. It doesn't feel right to us because, deep down we all know without a doubt we are all one. *Higher* has for eons represented outside of us and above. *Higher* is used in this case in reference to vibration. It isn't a reference to being above or better than. It is still a new concept for many, but we are all energy. And... all energy has a vibration. Some vibrations are higher than others, but all are of the same energy.

As the guidance shared, there are many names for the same thing. What you choose to call the all-knowing, never-ending part of you is perfect in all ways.

Michele's sharing of the colors of her energy streams helps us understand where our guides or trusted sources come from. They are the higher vibrations of our energy streams. As she said, these frequencies are given names so we can relate to them in a more physical or human way. This is not necessary, but it makes us feel better. We feel comfortable speaking with an Archangel or Ascended Master.

We all have access to this nonphysical, higher vibration part of our energy stream. It hasn't forgotten and is all-knowing, and much can be gained by contacting this available guidance.

> **Introspective Insights:**
> (Take a few minutes to journal or meditate on the following questions.)
> 1. How have you seen evidence of a connection with your Higher Self?
> 2. What do you call the nonphysical part of you, and how do you connect?
> 3. Are you familiar with the higher vibrations of your energy streams? How do you receive messages from them?
> 4. What are your thoughts and feelings on oneness and energy connections.?

Reason on Earth
(AC 16 Jan 24)

You have two reasons for choosing to come to the Earth plane. The first is that as a stream of universal energy, you came to Earth to experience the highest and lowest vibration of your stream and then expand it. Second, you came to fully live your Divine Intent, your mission, and make the difference you chose to make before your birth.

The Round Table, channeled by Vince Kramer

Knowing that our science tells us there are no mistakes or coincidences, I truly believe it is important for us all to know the reason we are here on this Earth. Can you share?

> Yes. This is something that will help each of you in living the life that you chose. We would like to share with all of you the important part you play in Universal Energy first off. Energy is not created or destroyed. It expands or contracts. The expansion of Universal Energy, which is the one and only energy, happens in the third and fourth dimensions. This means that expansion happens in and through you on your planet in the other third- and fourth-dimensional existences.

As we have shared in the past, each of you represents an energy stream or a combination of energy streams. You chose this stream that you represent. The life circumstances that you, the non-physical part of you, create and co-create allow you to experience the highest vibrations of your energy stream you can experience on Earth, and also the lowest vibrations. In the experience of the highs and lows, you expand the energy stream, thus expanding universal or source energy. This is the principal reason you chose to come to your Earth and live your life on the planet. Multidimensionally, this expansion happens in many ways.

Can you share how we experience expansion or how we can fully choose to expand?

When you say, "we," it is each of you on your planet. Know that each of you, as an energy stream, chose to be on Earth and live this life of expansion long before you were born. From the moment of that choice, all the pieces started to fall in place to support your choice. Part of the choice that was made was the difference you were going to make during your time on Earth.

We call this difference your Divine Intent. It is called many things. We refer to it in this manner because it is the intent that all the creations and co-creations of your Higher Self are based on. It is divine in that you chose this intent to support source energy and its expansion. Every creation and co-creation, every soul agreement in every detail, all lining up for you to make this difference that you chose to make.

In living the life that results in making this difference, you will find yourself in the highest vibrations you can hold in the third and fourth dimensions and expand the Universal Energy. It is truly an orchestrated concert of each being on your planet living your specific Divine Intent. Each person fully makes their difference; it allows others to do the same.

You can look at it as a giant puzzle. Each of you is a puzzle piece of the current existence on your planet, unique and not like another piece. When you live your Divine Intent and share it with others, you are putting your piece of the puzzle exactly where it belongs.

By doing this, you now make it possible for others to see where their puzzle piece fits in the wholeness of the puzzle, and they then live the life they are meant to live, making the difference they are meant to make. They are placing their piece in the puzzle, allowing others to see where their puzzle piece fits. As this happens, you experience the full spectrum of frequencies you can experience on Earth. You will move into the highest vibration of you and move beyond that vibration in each created and co-created experience.

This is the part that each of you plays in the wholeness of the Universe. Each level of your energy stream in every other stream, supporting the whole in every way, your higher selves, Divine Intents. Your guides, Divine Intents, are to support you in living this life and the expansion you create by living it fully.

In this now, Namaste.

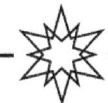

Michele's Musings

For over forty years, I had absolutely no idea why I was here on Earth. It didn't dawn on me that there had to be a reason. My belief in the early years was that God created us, and we were here to follow the rules and worship him. I confess that during these years, I frequented the wooden closet at the back of the church, with the priest's silhouette in the small, screened, sliding window hatch. I understood at the end of life, dependent on compliance levels, we await judgment, thumbs up or down. The hope being heaven, with Jesus and the angels. And then the sticky issue: What if my belief was in the wrong religion? I knew wonderful people in other religions and enjoyed parts of my own: stained glass, incense, the songs, etc., and my religion felt like *the* right one. How would I know for sure, though? The uncertainty was always in the back of my mind, especially when I took the Religions of the World university class. Other major religions had such devout followers, and some even had several gods. But I trusted my parents; I trusted the nuns; and I trusted the most well-read, smartest man I knew, my grandpa. If it was good enough for them, it was good enough for me, and for several decades of my life, I accepted this as the reason I was on Earth. Be good; if not, go to confession, then keep trying to earn your way to heaven.

This Active Connection shares a new perspective. It feels similar to team building. The completed puzzle is the team and the players all part of the team, playing different positions or in a work environment, each having different responsibilities and all for a common goal. We had a mission statement at work. New employees were familiar with our purpose, and our collective intent was to support people in changing substance-related choices. According to the guides, as part of the new paradigm we are raising our energetic frequency and making a difference through living our Divine Intent. As more and more people do this, we are collectively living the reason we came here on Earth, and with each puzzle piece in place, expanding the Universe's energy.

When I was researching the big questions, I enjoyed many of the tenets of the New Age movement, but I found the to-do list challenging. How much gunk can one person have, and how much fixing does a person need? I found there was not enough time in the day to clear the energy, cut the cords, and to be alert to bad energy lurking around every corner as well as emanating from other people. And at night, make note of your dreams as they happen and interpret them. Also, know your astrological chart, prepare for every inch of celestial rotation, and look out for Mercury in retrograde! The sky was constantly falling, and so was my energetic frequency. And I still needed more fixing.

Much of this did not feel like our reason for being on Earth. I felt I needed satiation from something grounding with a basis in science and something involving more gentleness and kindness toward ourselves especially. There had to be answers that connected science to empowering, higher vibration belief systems, including religions and the New Age. It is not that I need an easy way to live with easy answers. Still, the answers needed to make sense and, more importantly, be uplifting, liberating, and higher vibration and not disempowering.

I resonate with Vince and Mary's programs because they bring science and spirituality together in a way that the marriage makes sense. This is where I found the answers to why I am here and the greater purpose of human existence. And it came from inside of me, prompted by their wisdom and teachings that supported me in transforming numerous perceptions. The experience also satisfied my skepticism about channeling. It is not just a cool parlor trick to blindly believe and trust; it is explained by quantum physics and the energy of which we are all a part.

The Take a Quantum Leap program was literally a leap for me, especially once I got over the idea that retirement did not mean riding into the sunset as I had anticipated. And it was not all rosy. I found notes from one particular day where I listed my frustrations. I did not need or want to question my own thinking, and ironically, I prided myself on being a critical thinker, using my voice, and sticking to my guns. During the program, I found myself resisting the invitation to challenge long-held beliefs; I felt like I was being called out when I was challenged. I wanted to quit!

The default (comfy) ways of responding were near and dear to me, and the voice in my head was rearing its ugly head. I had thought for so long that I was thinking for myself. Really, I was seemingly content on autopilot and growling at the invitation to consider a different way of seeing myself and the world. I stewed and bristled at the feedback, which was impactful, of course, but the instability of questioning my own thinking was palpable and unnerving. I cried. Then I took a breath, journaled my frustration, and settled in to return for another day. I completed the program with a lovely working template of next steps and much more.

Within the program, I excavated my reason for being on Earth. Finding our purpose is one of the most asked questions nowadays.

I was so excited to nail it down, finally! And even more exciting, I had unknowingly made a career very related to my purpose; I had already been doing the work I came here to do, so nice! But there was more. During the seven-week process, I realized my Divine Intent for this life, the difference I am here to make, and how to do so. *(As a personal preference, I perceive the "divine" in Divine Intent as "sacred' or "of the very best kind" rather than "of God" or "godly," and various other meanings of the word.)*

The three parts of my purpose were brought to light: my quintessence is focused support, my gift is to bring the possibility of freedom by example and empowerment, to awaken others to their potential, and my Divine Intent is to empower others (and myself). It is through these three parts of me that I continue to make a difference in my life and in the lives of others and, in doing so, be part of the energetic expansion of the world.

In this Active Connection, the guides explain that we each represent our chosen energy streams, which are part of the main (the only) energy source, the whole puzzle. These streams, the nonphysical part of us, are our backup power generators, our supportive guides. It is my understanding that in our physical form, as we live the life we planned on Earth, we experience the spectrum of high frequency vibrations and low frequency vibrations of our energy streams (the ups and downs of everyday life). Living more fully in my higher vibration is the state of creating and co-creating, of expanding my energy and universal source energy. My quintessence is the energy I put out into the world, where I use my gifts and talents to live my Divine Intent, the road map, the blueprint to making a difference. And within our energy streams we tap into guidance as we maneuver more in the highest frequency emotions.

As humanity anticipates and participates in the evolution of and expansion into the new paradigm, we support the whole as we transform together from the *I consciousness* to the higher frequency *we consciousness*. Through this Active Connection, I understand more clearly that making a difference for and with others is key to living our Divine Intent fully, integrating our purpose into universal expansion and with it, our collective reason for being here.

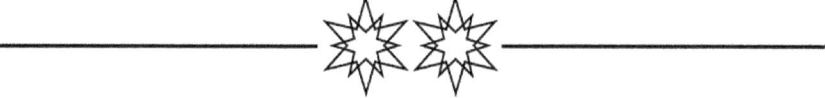

Vince and Mary's Reflections

The first paragraph of this guidance is sobering. We are at the leading edge of the Universal Energy expanding. It is all done in the third and fourth dimensions. That means we have truly chosen a very important mission. The discussion helps us see that we play a very important part in the oneness. The discussion around representing an energy stream or streams makes this life experience easier to grasp. If we just try to understand this concept at the highest levels, we can see the important role we have chosen.

Even when choosing to come to Earth, we are not alone. The Universe is conspiring to help us, and the higher vibrations (our guides) are always available to help us on our chosen journeys.

In an existence where maintaining our higher vibration is essential in creating the lives we are meant to live (including everything we want to create in our lives), it is important to recognize that making the difference we are meant to make is where we will live our highest vibration. Our programs help people do just that. It is the difference we are meant to make that helps us maintain our highest vibration.

We don't know about you, but we are excited about putting our pieces in this big puzzle.

In a Universe without right or wrong, Michele's first paragraph illustrates much of our confusion. So many rules have been shared with us. Our beliefs run deep because of the conviction of those who mean the most to us. What guidance is sharing doesn't go for or against any religion. It is an expanded view. It does force us to be open to more and to being more.

Along the way, we keep looking for the right way. We want the easiest way and the fastest way to make it happen. It is so important that we all realize that we have to find our way. It really isn't about learning more or someone else's way. It is truly about finding our way. We must live our way because that is the only way to deliver our Divine Intent to the world and expand Universal Energy according to our plan.

It is important for all of us to uncover, discover, and become aware of the reason we chose to come to Earth. When we can see it and feel it, we can't help but know we belong. No one talks about the three parts of purpose that Michele mentioned. Lots of people tell you how important it is to find your why, and just as many want to tell you *how* to find it. But there are three parts to your purpose: the who, what, and why. That is the full reason you are on Earth.

Introspective Insights:
(Take a few minutes to journal or meditate on the following questions.)

1. Where have you taken on the beliefs of others and limited your life?
2. What would life be like if you were making the difference you were meant to make?
3. How can you help your children or grandchildren not forget what they obviously remember?
4. How can you help them develop beliefs that support and empower them?

Earth Transformation
(AC 15 Nov 23)

The cycles of evolution have been experienced throughout the eons and throughout every corner of the Universe. The stages are well known and all of you on Earth at this time chose to be during this stage. The movement from "I" to "we" is in progress. You wanted to be part of this transformation.

The Round Table, channeled by Vince Kramer

Shall we talk about the movement of energy right now toward supporting a transformation?

> The movement into oneness is the transformation. As a planet moves into oneness, there is an experience of magnified duality. What this means is duality in itself becomes fractured. It is like the competing parts breaking up into the smallest units before there is a coming together once again of all the parts.
>
> Let us give you an example that you can see in the world right now. The politics in your country are quite divided and are becoming more and more so over time. The division between the two parties is quite evident, but you all are witnessing a split or a fissure in each party that is widening and widening.

There are actually many, and there will be many more. This would seem to be created by an energy that is vibrating at separation, but it is quite the opposite. The movement is away from the divisive groups and inward. This will move each individual toward self and can be the precursor for their self-acceptance and reliance. This will make the transition to the *we consciousness* an easier one for most.

What is being experienced with this energetic shift is the awareness of how much each person is locked into their own specific ways and the belief that their way is the only true way. Up to this point in time, people have come together in concentrated groups that believe and think the same. These groups support each other in the separation. As these groups become fractured, each individual will face a lack of support for those beliefs they hold that have kept them in separation. They will begin to notice that even in their groups, they have felt alone.

In this new level of awareness, there will be an energetic movement toward understanding that you all are the same, even in your uniqueness. You all desire the mutual experience of support and community. You all require it to find your growth and expansion in the support of others. You all will have the opportunity to fully live your Divine Intent in support of others, which will, in turn, support your understanding and movement into a more empowered unity of self. This will be the collective move toward oneness, a move toward unity.

In this now, Namaste.

Michele's Musings

There was a time not long ago in this Canadian's life when I was familiar with several CNN news anchors, Fox News anchors, and some MSNBC. I enjoyed watching the satirists on late-night talk shows, splaying the absurdity and corruption in political interviews that I had enjoyed alongside news network interviews. From a neighboring country, I cheered on my favorites during the last two

United States elections. I was immersed and vicariously frustrated at the time, depending on the winners and losers. It may sound shameful, but I was more familiar with what was going on south of the border than I was with Canadian politics. Then I quit—cold turkey.

The breakup has lasted two years, and I have no regrets. I am grateful for the shift in my personal energy, not being plugged into the fight, into the mistruths, into the all-around low vibrational nastiness. I remain aware, though, of the clanging duality. According to the guides in this Active Connection, duality is a good sign of the unfolding process, the move toward oneness. It initially sounded contradictory, but then it was explained further. There is much hope in learning that each individual moves away from divisiveness toward unity and oneness.

The energetic movement mentioned in the Active Connection describes our uniqueness and our sameness. Does oneness imply sameness? I see it this way: My Divine Intent is unique, but what we all want is similar. And that is to experience support and community. My personality is such that I can refuel my system only by being away from people. I am an introvert. Crowds are not my jam at all. I love music concerts, but soon into the entertainment, my central nervous system says, "Stop!" With family gatherings, no matter the fun, the card games, the laughter, and the sense of community, there is a tipping point when I know that I am done. No matter the amount of support, enjoyment, and love, I will excuse myself or discreetly move to more quiet ground. I am different from others, but we want similar things in our lives, and we are collectively one.

Now, if I had only one or the other, solitude or community, I would surely miss the other. I remember the feeling of being shunned when my first marriage ended. *Shunned* sounds harsh but it was how I felt at the time. My family had no idea about the complex layers behind the decision or the reasons it did not work out. I realized some of these myself only decades later. They loved my partner and were saddened when their grandchildren's home had the unfortunate designation of being a broken one. After all, marriage is for life, sanctioned by the church. The separation was followed by months of involuntary solitude. I was alone. I was with my children part-time, but as an adult, I felt a prolonged sting of loneliness. I was also guilt-ridden, perpetuated by silence from a large family. It was through this challenging time that I realized how important and vital support and community are. It is often within the experience of being without that we learn how critical our social connections are. As we lived through the acute phase of the recent global pandemic, the thirst for connection was palpable, and we continue to feel the fallout of unexpected disconnect and deeply felt separateness. My heart goes out to the innumerable people who live with loneliness daily and often for years.

My career was spent in the helping field, specifically, as mentioned earlier, mostly around problematic substance use and in a correctional institutional setting. The clients were sentenced to the facility with substance-related offenses, the majority being for driving while impaired. Earlier in my career, while in the federal system, substance-related offenses ranged from assault causing bodily harm, domestic abuse, general violent offenses, drunk driving offenses, and others. I worked with human beings experiencing the worst times of their lives. Separation from family and society is the cost of choices, usually perpetrated directly against others, especially connected to substance use and/or mental health issues. This Active Connection helps me to imagine if I had made similar choices with incarceration being the result and how lack of freedom, negative, low frequency environment, fear, and loneliness would have consumed me, even in a small facility. I shuddered to imagine making a huge federal prison my home.

I guess it was with that motivation, that sense, that I kept assisting in some way, not just for the paycheck, and for the sake of the safety of our communities, but also out of a level of compassion for the day-to-day isolation of these people from their families and communities. I honestly believed that we could assist in making a difference in the quality of their lives if we could help them see themselves differently. The only testament to our efficacy was the numbers that never returned to prison, though many did. And if we remained true to our mission statement, we would, without judgment, begin our work with them again and again and again.

My underlying belief during my career was that people could change their behavior, but we had to create an environment conducive to them considering behavior change. I believed people could change because I had changed many things about myself and my behavior over my lifetime. I had also seen others change. I witnessed transformation in people. I observed the transformation that occurs when we help others make different choices and see themselves in new ways that are empowering and healing. Eventually, ideally, people resolve trauma, commit to self-care, and go on to care for their families and communities after release.

I witnessed the result of duality and separateness in institutional settings, the silent screams of desperation when suicide was perceived as the final relief to never-ending internalized suffering and emotional pain. I also saw the callousness and apathy of colleagues, indicating just another layer of internal protection for otherwise compasionate and kind people who chose a career working with people in confinement, humans locked up and at their worst. I was not an innocent bystander of similar attitudes or the beliefs of a subculture that often mirrors the separation of the larger population: we and them, good and bad, rich and poor, a constant state of duality. And yes, I am very aware that there are consequences to criminal choices and that societal safety is paramount. It is also true that the sentence is the punishment, so what is in our families' and communities', and their own best interest while in jail? Maybe they will change, or maybe they will not, but the chance of change increases depending on the environment and time spent learning how to do so.

I will always remember the brisk fall morning later in my career when a young man, not yet in his twenties, arrived at the front door of the small facility. His mom was helping carry his belongings. They said goodbye at the front entrance, and she left the building. I was leaving for lunch shortly after. When I turned the corner toward my car, I saw her sitting in the driver's seat of her truck with her head in her hands. As I got closer, I could see that she was sobbing. She opened her window as she noticed my approach. Her heart was breaking. Her son had never been to jail. She was terrified for him. My heart broke for her. At that moment, I understood so well that if it were one of my sons, I would not be so different. I reassured her that he would be okay and that he would be supported throughout treatment. I explained that even though the facility was technically a jail, the emphasis was on supporting and helping people to empower themselves, to understand their choices, and to make positive changes in their lives.

When I trained new employees, I emphasized that the offenders (we referred to them as clients because it was also a treatment facility) were someone's mom, dad, son, daughter, etc. We were responsible not just to support and assist, but also to be role models of respect and appropriate communication in all interactions, no matter the job title. Ideally, it was a subculture of nonduality, support, and community. Every day brought various challenges, but the underlying philosophy was one of working together for the greater good. After all, eventually, most offenders are released to the communities of which we and our families are a part.

We look different, we act different, and we seem to be very different from each other, but at a high frequency, people have a common desire: We want support, community, and the best for ourselves and others. At a less conscious level, on autopilot, most still want, at the very least, the best for themselves and their families. Based on what the guides have shared, it would seem that our Divine Intents, the reasons for being here, and the difference we are here to make are unique to each of us. Does uniqueness mean different? And can we simultaneously want the same things but be different individuals? I have gradually grown to believe we are all unique sparks of the same energy source. As we live our Divine Intents, the outcome of that is woven into the movement toward the energetic expansion of the Universe, to the unfolding new paradigm, to oneness.

There is hope in each of the Active Connections, but this one has a pointedness. It feels more essential to experience the hope and anticipation of moving toward support and community even if we are not witnessing it in our communities or our own lives at the moment, especially in the never-ending reels of war, political chaos, and divisiveness. This understanding brings with it hope to hang onto and movement toward a deeper level of knowing, acceptance, and appreciation.

Vince and Mary's Reflections

This guidance gives us hope. As we look at our world right now, the chaos is concerning. It seems we get further and further apart. Hearing that the divisiveness we are experiencing at the degree we are experiencing is actually a sign that we are coming out of it brings hope. We believe it is important to hear that much of what we see is a mirror for each of us to look inside to see where we are divided or an invitation to see where we have judgment on parts of ourselves—even where we treat parts of ourselves like outcasts. It is a reminder that the work is an inside job, and we are responsible for our part.

Michele illustrates how we can all get caught up in the energy of the collective and, in turn, contribute to that collective energy. Separating ourselves from that energy can be a valid first step, but lasting change—or the more desired transformation—must include the part of us that has been mirrored to us. It is as she says: "We are different and the same at the exact same time." There is duality even in saying, "I am this, but not that." It is an internal duality that is reflected to us in what we attract. It also contributes to the duality of the collective.

The concepts of mirrors and projections are instrumental in understanding these new paradigm concepts. The differences that we choose to see are the ones that foster duality. We aren't saying ignore the perception of difference, but more accurately, notice the perception and do the internal work to change the belief that is responsible for the perception. When we see one that we perceive is broken or we want to fix, we are fostering the duality.

There truly is hope. And we are the hope. As we find those parts of ourselves that we have judgment about, learn to accept that we are these things and then love them unconditionally. We become the energy of the oneness that is presented in the guidance. When we have no judgment on self, we remove our judgment on others. When we realize, as science shares, that there is no right or wrong, we remove the need for separation.

Introspective Insights:
(Take a few minutes to journal or meditate on the following questions.)

1. How are you experiencing this Earth's transformation?
2. Where are you seeing the duality in yourself?
3. Where do you see you are locked into your beliefs now, where your way is the only way?
4. Where do you see proof in your daily life that this transformation is happening?

Navigating the World
(AC 16 Nov 23)

You are the creator of your life, the creator of your reality. Your choices are the deciding factors in your life. If you master your mind and choose thoughts in alignment with who you are and why you are on Earth, your journey will be straight and smooth. Remember though, each diversion brings a gift to help you make a bigger difference.

The Round Table, channeled by Vince Kramer

You have shared about the world and how we might experience it. Can you share how to navigate it?

> In this now, there doesn't need to be anything you do to navigate anything. If you choose, you can hold your vibration and not be part of anything to do with the chaos your world is experiencing. You can choose to be the observers of it and see it for what it is, or you can see it in a negative way and be pulled into it and, in turn, create chaos in your life.
>
> When we say you can see it for what it is, this is what it is. It is a part of the process of transforming your world into unity. If you choose to see the experiences of this transformation from that under-

standing, you won't get wrapped up in the spiral of others in the transformation. You won't be affected by the chaos and the low vibrations created by it. Life can be vibrant, happy, and full of those things that best support you in all you want to do and in all you are meant to be.

Thank you. How do we best do that?

You energetically know what is happening, and we have shared with you what is happening. So, on the inside and the outside, you understand what you are experiencing around you with your 3D senses. If you acknowledge the greater separation as part of the process, you will see it for what it is and not be affected by it. If, as the observer, you see it for what it is and know that it is taking you all where you have chosen to go, your reality will be the movement toward oneness inside of you and outside of you.

You will have a life that fully supports you and who you are. You will find opportunities and experience life in a positive and empowered way in your observation from your higher vibration. Your reality will be positive, joyful, and rewarding. But, as you know, if you allow your vibration to drop and observe from a low vibrational, victim perspective, full of fear, your reality will be hopeless, full of despair, and leave you feeling disempowered, out of control, and a victim. We know it might sound too easy, but it does come down to your choice. How is it said? "Life is what you make it." We want to remind you what you get is aligned with your thoughts and feelings.

See the current and future chaos as the steps of the process that are getting you closer to the collective living in oneness and celebrate it. Live your life in the happy, joyful state of knowing who you are and why you are here.

In this now, Namaste.

Michele's Musings

Truly, we have traveled some distance together, and I would enjoy sharing this co-creative process briefly and how it relates to navigating the world. First, as I listen to each Active Connection, I could say it is sort of like Christmas morning, but personally, I enjoy Easter more; not so much the earlier-than-necessary mornings, but little faces filled with anticipation of the search for eggs and other treats, the dawning of spring after a long, frigid winter, and the smells of oven-roasted turkey, filled with stuffing, wafting through the house, teasing our taste buds throughout the day. Also, leading up to Easter we are not subjected to (or volunteers of) long shopping hours, with busy stores and frenzied people, spending copious amounts of money on things not needed, with purchases on stretched-to-the-limit credit cards.

So, yes, each Active Connection is like Easter morning to me. What will I uncover on this day that will expand my thinking and raise my energy? What old beliefs will the guides' words chisel away to reveal a remembering of sorts of an expanded, perceived self, life, and the world? The creative process raises my energetic vibration and reminds me daily of another analogy: panning for gold. Initially, the television show *Storage Wars* came to mind, which I enjoyed years ago. The excitement was in the anticipation of finding treasures, but the frequency was much lower, first because it is a scripted TV show and second because the units most likely belonged to either deceased people or people who could not pay rent. Panning for gold is adventurous in nature, and it involves the anticipation of riches, but the vibration would be much higher than a rather *unreal* reality TV show.

Anyway, veering back to this high frequency creative process: First, I listen to the recording, then I read through a printed paper copy and circle the words and phrases that jump out, and with that, I have stories from lived experiences, some fun and, as you have seen, some not-so-fun. As I am co-creating this project, I am taking one of Vince and Mary's programs. The concept at this moment of writing is about being conscious of energy and emotional states and attuning our vibration to a higher frequency of emotions toward contentment, hopefulness, positiveness, eagerness, happiness, joy, etc. And not just attuning to move up to a better feeling state but also to whatever and whoever that higher (or lower) frequency aligns with or attracts to me. As I finish each section, I breathe out a celebratory sigh of completion and relief but also a ping of vulnerability. What I choose to share, no matter the silliness or seriousness, comes from an open, optimistic heart and a high vibration of gratitude for this co-creative opportunity. This is my understanding of the crux of navigating the world.

This Active Connection, the continuation from Earth transformation, responds to the question of how we can more easily navigate the movement toward oneness, that space between the trapezes, of letting go of one way of perceiving but not yet grasping or understanding the next transition of life on Earth. It is one thing to say yes, I acknowledge what is occurring, and another to have the knowledge of how to maneuver through the instability en route to the expansion. The guides share seemingly easy and helpful ways to avoid spiraling into chaos. The part about what will happen if we choose to get absorbed by it felt unsettling at first as my energetic vibration dropped near fear, reading it for the first time. My focus, for some reason, went right to my family and to losing what I perceived as a comfortable and relatively stable life.

When the guides explain how to navigate chaos or a potentially challenging transformation, the first step is to understand that separateness and chaos are part of the new paradigm process. Then, we hold our vibration and avoid being drawn into the lower vibrations of despair, hopelessness, and fear.

How relieving to hear we have a choice in what can, at first glance, seem daunting. It is great news! We can *choose* to hold a higher vibrational energy state. So here are some of my go-tos when things get dicey or low vibe: I listen to music with uplifting melodies and words; I play the guitar and sing, not because I am particularly good at either, but because both make me feel good; I have a bath, not because I am dirty but because it feels good; I write, not because I am particularly good at it, but it makes me feel good; I put essential oils in my diffuser because certain scents make me feel good; I walk in nature every day, weather permitting; I have a delicious snack and a glass of wine; I connect with fun people. You get the message.

And there are more ways to raise my frequency, especially when I add my words, thoughts, and other people to the mix. And it is not always easy. A fun, quick example: One of my brothers texted us last evening. We live at the same lake, and he could see through his telescope that a moose was stuck in the ice. We have all seen videos of moose rescues, cheering for the successful carving out of the ice, and a huge, beautiful animal pulled to safety. I could see the faint outline of the animal from my front window, just slightly moving, probably exhausted but struggling to stay above water. It was getting dark. We knew we would not be able to sleep knowing it was out there. But the ice had been melting, and it could be disastrous for my husband to ride out on the quad to assess the situation. He could drown, and even if he did not, how could he pull out a thousand-pound moose on his own?

Anyway, I implored him to take a life jacket or at least a floatie noodle so if he went through the ice he could float temporarily until help arrived, but he was out the door. I heard the quad start. My heart was pounding! I loved the moose, but I loved him more! We had just retired and moved to a lake house that he built; if he drowned, how could I manage on my own? I had read too many stories of people drowning after breaking through thinning ice. I watched the quad cruising across the slushy ice. It kept moving forward above the ice, thank goodness! Then he turned away from the form I could see struggling, and the quad veered off to an area close to the nearby island. OMG! The ice was too thin! He had to abort! But now, where was he going? How would he get home? I could no longer see the quad!

My phone rang. It was him. The form we could see from our window was a large tree branch someone had put on the ice. The "struggling moose" was the branches slightly blowing in the wind. Yes, the spiral happened so automatically, with a plethora of low vibrational thoughts and emotions. The funny thing is, there *was* a moose, but it was farther away, toward the island where the quad had headed. And it was not stuck in the ice. He or she was just chilling out on the ice for a spell until an annoying human on a noisy machine disturbed his or her slumber. I, on the other hand, allowed my thoughts and emotions to go to the worst-case scenarios, hence functioning at a very low vibration and very stuck in the chaos.

The guides explain that we can choose differently regarding our energy and the move through chaotic or transitioning emotional times, that we can choose to realize the transition for what it is and be observers of it, from a state of higher frequency energy, not bothered by it, not lowering our vibration to meet it. When my thoughts acknowledge we are headed exactly where we are pointed toward on the map, driving right past the towns of separateness, divisiveness, and chaos toward the new paradigm destination city of oneness, support, and community, I hold the frequency of anticipation, appreciation, positive expectation, and optimism, and my experience will attune to and align with that lovely frequency.

The road can be less (or more) bumpy, and it is up to us—which again, is good and bad news. There exist the clamoring subpersonalities, the voices in our heads that we can leg wrestle with each day as they taunt us with worst-case scenarios or tell us that we are not worthy, not attractive, not smart, getting too old for relevance, not good enough, etc. (I am remembering *Saturday Night Live's* Stuart Smalley. Yes, it was funny years ago, but the downside was an unhelpful mockery of mastering our minds, taking control of our thoughts, emotions, and lives while raising our emotions to higher energetic frequencies.)

I have learned through Vince and Mary's programs that when things get bumpy (unless a moose is involved), my intention is to choose a new thought, sometimes related to the low frequency ones associated with put-downs and what ifs, and sometimes, without bypassing the actual feelings or emotions around the issue, I take myself somewhere completely different. And I win the leg wrestle. A loud, recent example is my health, specifically the pain in my body when I open my eyes in the morning. I can start my day by saying to myself, "This is so shitty! I hate my body! This will never get better! I don't want to get up!" or I can start the day saying, "Holy shit, my body hurts this morning! Yes, I feel you, and yes, I can breathe through it a bit, and yes, I can move, and yes, I can enjoy this beautiful view on this warm spring day."

Positive self-talk is nothing new, but this way of utilizing positive self-talk is more relevant and realistic. With increased awareness and intention, I transform my frustration, negativity, and victimhood about a debilitating physical condition into a day of hopefulness, optimism, and even some appreciation for spring's arrival.

Now imagine this being our default emotional state: empowering ourselves, mastering our minds and emotions, having feelings of optimism, hopefulness, enthusiasm, and knowing without any doubt who we are and why we are here. Imagine a movement toward oneness that will be felt and integrated inside and around us, living fully what we had planned and connecting and supporting each other. And best of all, we get to decide; we get to choose it and continue to choose it each day as we do all the things that make us feel good, that raise our frequency to match and attract everything that we want in this life, no matter the chaos around us or within us. And in so doing, we uniquely assist others in doing the same.

Vince and Mary's Reflections

Although the first statement from guidance was difficult to grasp, it brings hope. It frees us from just experiencing the world around us. It helps us see we never lost the power or the ability to choose our life and how we perceive it. Do you feel the freedom in that statement?

It can be very difficult to see the chaos in the world as part of the process. We expect to see things get better, not worse, before we see a change or transformation. This is where trust and surrender come in: Trust that the situation needs to get worse so it can get better. It is truly a new concept that we change our lives by changing our perception and where we put our attention. We are navigating our inner self, not the outer world. This is easier done if we see the chaos as a move in the right direction.

Michele supports our understanding of this guidance in her example of the moose. If we act and react on our perceptions or our judgments, we are not only caught up in the chaos, but also, we *become* the chaos. Our free will is so powerful and important in this human experience. She also illustrates where and how we can find freedom from the craziness our minds have learned to participate in.

Guidance isn't promoting or even suggesting positive self-talk. It is about moving into your highest vibration and maintaining it. It is about using the concepts of energy. Do not allow the energy of others to pull you into a lower vibration, a vibration of chaos. Then, learn that you can hold your higher vibration, and use the understanding of entrainment to support others, raising their vibration. This will help them step out of the chaos instead of pulling you into it.

Introspective Insights:

(Take a few minutes to journal or meditate on the following questions.)

1. Where have you been pulled into the chaos surrounding you?
2. How can you be more aware of where you have contributed to the lower vibration?
3. Where have your thoughts pulled you into the problem instead of keeping you on the outside?
4. How can your life be better by trusting that there are no mistakes or coincidences?

Universal Knowledge
(AC 20 Dec 23)

After choosing your reason for incarnating on the Earth plane as a strand of universal energy, you came to believe that you were disconnected from everything. As you chose to forget, you no longer believed you had access to all the knowledge of the universe. Nothing could be further from the truth. All the knowledge of the universe is available to you. All you have to do is ask.

The Round Table, channeled by Vince Kramer

We humans have access to so much information, yet most don't know we can tap into this universal knowledge. Can you share about this?

> Yes, of course. There are many reasons that, as you say, humans don't access this knowledge and information available to them. First, they just don't know because of the need to forget. Second, it is uncomfortable to go against society's beliefs. There has been much confusion, fear, and control around connecting with this information and guidance.
>
> Over the years, this has been made taboo or something only special people could do. Over the centuries, it has been taught that

this type of connection was for the chosen few. This has caused separation and, in many ways, has been used to control people. This resulted in society forgetting this information can be accessed, leaving more and more people not being taught how to access it or the possibility of accessing it never presented. This then resulted in more and more people not even knowing it could be accessed.

What is there to access? What is available to us?

All-knowingness is available, every thought that has ever been thought, every idea that has ever been had, the answers to all the questions of who, what, why, how, where, when... It is all available. But know that it takes, first, a knowing it is there and can be accessed, second, a willingness to access your answers, and third, a belief that you can access some information.

There are large groups of people stuck at each of these junctures in accessing this universal knowledge. Those who don't know it is there have several obstacles in their way. Their parents and influential people in their lives didn't know the information was available; or worse, they believe it is wrong or maybe even evil to access it. Those who aren't willing to access it have many reasons that they have justified not accessing it.

Some of the reasons are: "It won't work for me." "It is too hard to get answers." "I don't know if I'm making it up." And, of course, the reason for much of the resistance in your world, "I don't have time." Those who don't believe that it is possible or believe they are wrong if they do access it are stuck in the old beliefs created over the years from fear or the desire to control others. It is important for all of you to know and understand that beliefs aren't real; they are ideas that you choose to believe and use to govern your life. You can choose other ones, and that can truly set you free from the beliefs that have been limiting you.

In this now, Namaste.

Michele's Musings

I love the idea of setting myself free from the beliefs that disempower, being open to endless possibilities, living life fully on purpose, connecting with, and trusting nonphysical guidance. Who wouldn't, right? Well, according to this Active Connection, most people don't. But many are just unaware that it is there. As you are reading this and hopefully experiencing expanded perception in various areas of your life, you are indeed among the extraordinary minority.

The guides share the main types, but one I have experienced that I find most ironic and interesting is those who tap in regularly and do not recognize it as nonphysical guidance. I happen to live with someone who does this. My husband would never use words like *third eye*, *chakras*, *awakening*, *expansion*, or *energy frequency*. Still, he understands that solutions to problems he encounters while doing construction projects, fixing things, etc., surface in his mind as he drifts off to sleep or just as he wakes up. He would never refer to this as tapping into universal knowledge. He is perceptive, highly intuitive, and has a keen bullshit meter. He imagines or envisions projects, including significant year-long construction endeavors, and completes them as a master creator would, even though he would not be at all interested in what the notion of connecting is. He is a true example of the Law of Attraction without knowledge of the concept. He did enjoy *The Matrix,* so we have discussed his superpowers in those terms. And it is true, he can fix almost anything. Over the years, outside of his full-time career, he renovated and built homes without being taught how to do such things. He has an uncanny ability to look at various appliances or mechanical things and know how to repair them. I tease as I reference the possibility of past-life skill sets, to which he responds with the usual eye roll.

Universal Knowledge

He talks about the things he is grateful for every day and often expresses how he truly loves his life. It is higher-frequency energy at its finest! He has his not-so-good days, but mostly, he lives a tuned in, expanded life without naming it as such.

Before my growth experiences with Vince and Mary, I had learned in numerous courses that our guidance and our waking up come from inside us. Still, I did not understand it in a pragmatic way or in a way that is helpfully applicable to day-to-day living. I did not believe it or integrate it into a meaningful practice of connecting with nonphysical energy. My reasons are similar to what the Active Connection describes: various conditioning by the usual suspects mentioned. I do not recall, during the formative years, ever hearing the message that our guidance and wisdom are inside us. I may have been absent from that religion class, or I may have missed the pulpit sermon. Still, the message I *do* recall was to seek and follow soul-saving wisdom, to ask for needed absolution, and to acknowledge the guidance and acceptance from outside of us.

I eventually began to accept the connection between science and the numinous, that everything is energy, and it *all* comes from inside. Still, it has taken time to recognize and replace automatic beliefs and to know we are always connected, even if on autopilot. To make matters stickier, in the early years after releasing remnants of religious indoctrination, I thought and believed that the goal was to ascend out of ourselves, and that spiritual awakening meant transcending our third-dimensional human nature. I was attracted to this idea, perhaps because in my experience, going within has not always been a pleasant trip. Being alone with my thoughts can be alarming and disarming. I am still learning what solitude is and what it feels like to experience stillness. I have a lot behind me that can be daunting if I indulge, and I hopefully still have much time ahead, but I have tended to allow my thoughts to veer into the future, often fearing the worst. With the more recent learning and coaching, and with these Active Connections, being in the present moment is a reprieve. I can breathe and tune in to the *moments* the guides have mentioned often, which is essential; it is all there is.

So yes, guides, Trusted Source, angels, Ascended Masters, etc., are references to nonphysical energy that sound like entities outside of us. Still, it is all energy, even within the smallest particles of our physical makeup or our nonphysical higher frequency. We are a part of the main energy source, AND we are seemingly solid third-dimensional beings. I mentioned energy streams in other chapters, and whether we believe it or not, I am convinced more than ever that we all choose what energy stream(s) we are a part of in this life. And we live our 3D lives experiencing the frequencies along the continuum of low-to-high frequency energies, low-vibe emotions to high-vibe emotions. We tune into ourselves, not to any outside beings, and connect to all-knowingness, to everything we ever wanted to know. How fun that we can internally google universal knowledge anytime, anywhere, and for anything we want answers to or guidance for.

I am not there yet, not consistently anyway, but what occurs as I soak in the words of the Active Connection is a significantly expanded view of the world and life in general. Initially, it was more challenging to grasp the higher-frequency information, but as I practiced raising my emotional state, I experienced a very moving inner transformation. Since the early part of this writing, I have been participating in Vince and Mary's Accelerate Your Purpose program. With these growth activities in tandem, it is an interesting immersion that satisfies my existential queries and, at the same time, chips away old belief systems, residual skepticism, and doubt. Gratefully, the consequence is a higher frequency default energy, and I am finally loosening my grip on what I thought was real and beginning to trust my inner guidance. Amen to that!

In my day-to-day world, I enjoy numerous opportunities to share what I am up to, and it usually begins with people asking about retirement. We moved recently from an acreage near a city out to a remote area of the province to a lake house my husband built over the past year. The curiosity is related to how we keep busy while being so isolated. Here is the usual conversation:

"So, Michele, what are you up to? What are you keeping busy at since retirement?"

I usually respond, "I'm enjoying retirement, especially loving not having to wake up to an alarm." I then share that I am writing.

"Awesome! What are you writing about?"

There it is! How do I explain something so complex, perception-altering, and extraordinary? Attempting to explain the new paradigm could not possibly do it justice.

And I cautiously respond, "Umm err umm, I am sharing my perspective, through stories of lived experiences, related to all sorts of cool, relevant human life questions, answered by guides who are a source of nonphysical energy, umm sort of."

And for those on a similar path as me, I relate what Vince does as similar to a woman named Esther Hicks and how she connects with nonphysical energy she refers to as Abraham. That likeness elicits understanding and usually interest.

For the majority, though, I attempt to satisfy sideways looks and go on to explain the similarities between what I am speaking about and *The Matrix* movie. I associate Vince with the main character, Neo, as I tell them Vince plugs into Universal Energy just like Neo—well, almost like Neo. I have usually lost them long before *The Matrix* analogy. For the lovely few who politely stay tuned, they usually at some point, at the very least, acknowledge that we all relate to some experience of a gut sense, spider sense, or a vague, intuitive knowing. That is a start, right?

Some Active Connections are similar to others but without redundancy. Learning first that the connection exists, then that we are able to access and trust it—especially after challenging conditioning and old belief systems—takes repetition and practice as with any muscle strengthening. Understanding also deepens with repetition and practice. I am not adept, but I am experiencing growth. I have cool tools, and I feel a gentle transformation. When I get distracted with what I used to call "real life," I slide into autopilot, and my car is without a driver for as long as it takes to be aware again and move back into the driver's seat. The difference for me now, though, is that "real life" is more of an expanded state; it is all of it, the whole spectrum of low and high frequency experiences, and I keenly feel when I am not in alignment with higher energetic states or my purpose for this lifetime.

Writing almost daily, connected to the high frequency information of the guides through Vince's Active Connections, keeps me conscious of my energetic vibration, not in a hypervigilant way, but in a way that says, "Wow, interesting how I'm reacting to that." Or "Wow, I really feel low today; I am choosing to change that." The best part is the umpteen ways that I *choose* to change my thoughts and my emotional state and raise my frequency back to one higher up the scale to at least contentment or optimism.

I have mentioned that I am a work in progress. I like slow and gradual, and with time and practice, I am learning to trust my inner guidance as not being an entity *out there*, but a trusted, beloved, dear friend, ever a part of me, connected as *one* to the main source of love, of Universal Energy.

Vince and Mary's Reflections

This isn't the first session that we have heard we have access to universal knowledge. But this is the first time they have tied believing and understanding to what we have been taught because of the taboo placed on it. Society's fears and doubts constantly result in more and more people giving up a gift because others say it is wrong or point out it was for only the special or ordained. In many ways, it became a lost art because no one was taught to or encouraged to connect.

It is exciting and encouraging to know that so much is actually available to us. It is empowering to know that we have all the answers to every who, what, why, how, where, and when and the fact that we just need to ask the question and listen for the answers. It is also comforting to know that most of us weren't taught because our parents didn't know themselves. We can stop this trend by learning to connect and then sharing with others. I find it important that guidance shared with us through Active Connection the many reasons people doubt their own connection. Just knowing relieves some of the resistance.

Michele's sharing about her husband and their connection helps us see that more of us tap into guidance than we think. Guidance is always available and coming to us. We just might not recognize it or pay attention to it. If we realized that much of what we experience is supported by higher vibrations, we would be much further along.

Michele's understanding that the guidance we receive comes from the outside is indicative of the separation we have been taught and seemingly experience in the third dimension. When we come to understand and believe we are all one energy, it is easier to accept that it is an inside job. It then makes sense that our earthly experience isn't transcending out of our bodies; we are already multi-dimensional.

Michele powerfully shares her experiences, and we can all see from her example that it is all a journey of growth and expansion supported by trust and surrender. We are all on a journey. We are living our personal journeys together.

Introspective Insights:

(Take a few minutes to journal or meditate on the following questions.)

1. How would your life be different if you freely allowed guidance into your life?
2. Where has what you think you know been challenged in an empowering way?
3. What questions would you ask if you allowed yourself to believe you have access to all the answers?
4. What would happen if you were to accept that we are all the same energy with access to all-knowingness?

Either/Or
(AC 24 Jan 24)

Everything exists in the Universe. There is no separation. The true evolution in every civilization on every planet is the understanding and the movement into this new paradigm principle. There is only oneness and unity. You all must heal the duality and separation in self to support the whole move into one.

The Round Table, channeled by Vince Kramer

You talk often about it not being an either/or world or Universe. Can you share what you mean by either/or? And if our world isn't either/or, what is it?

> This is an excellent question, and understanding the answer can be life-changing. At the same time, it can move your world closer to the consciousness we share. The concept has explanations in both science and spirituality.
>
> We will explain the concept that covers both. We have been discussing with you over the years the duality and separateness and moving into unity and oneness. This is the foundation for understanding the answers to your questions. The duality or separateness that you and others are experiencing in your lives is nothing but an

illusion. This illusion is supported by your five senses and the collective beliefs of the Earth inhabitants in this now. We can share more about the illusion at another time.

This duality is what sets up the belief that it or everything is either this way or that way. The duality shows itself as either good or bad, right or wrong, for me or against me. This shows up in even more challenging and counterproductive ways, such as my way being the right way and your way being the wrong way. You are either with me, or you are against me; you agree with me, or you are wrong. This way of thinking and acting is the cause of the separation you are observing and experiencing in your world and country right now.

This way of thinking has created great divides between countries, citizens, and even families; believing everything has to be one way or the other accentuates the belief that you are separate from others and creates the illusion that those people affect or, even worse, control your life. The tendency is to become more protective of your beliefs and your truth and reject others. This either/or existence in your world has been the impetus for all the wars you have experienced and read about. The belief that I have to support and defend my way has been catastrophic. We will share with you that everything exists in Universal Energy.

There is no *one* way. The Universe is and/both. It is both your way *and* my way. Nothing is good or bad. It just is, all based on the perception of who is observing it. And this perception comes from a set of beliefs that each individual has accepted or formed, based on their experiences and the interpretation of them. This all means that it is your way *and* my way, and neither is more right or wrong.

Moving into the new paradigm supporting the *we consciousness* requires that you accept each way is true without judgment and work together to find our way. Finding our way will eliminate war, poverty, and all things associated with the duality experienced and promoted in your world in this now. It will free you all to experience heaven on Earth.

In this now, Namaste.

Michele's Musings

This is new to me. And might I say, almost too abstract to comprehend. There is really no wrong or right, good or bad, and no either/or. Everything is *and*, and *both*? How's that? It kind of takes the wind out of my sails: Nothing to defend; nothing to prove, to argue about, to be right about. There is actually a candy coating of freedom in that, especially for someone who needs certainty and to know what is correct and what is not. But what about fighting for trans rights, women's rights, and the rights of other minorities? What about child trafficking? Is there no right and wrong in those scenarios? Do we just go about our days willy-nilly? Do we stand for nothing? Do we not have strong opinions about things, especially related to human rights?

You may be able to tell this is where the rug gets pulled out from under me. Am I just so conditioned for right and wrong, for separation and duality? I am definitely against whoever stole my son's identity a year ago and all the havoc that wreaked. The faceless, nameless criminal was wrong, and if you are not with me on that, you are wrong as well, right? What would the new paradigm look like in that scenario? What would *we consciousness* look like?

Does it mean that everything is peachy? That we created it all, that we planned it all before we were born, including the good, the bad, the horrific? Suppose I was to believe and trust the guides in this Active Connection, fully sit with this vision of a new paradigm that is kumbaya, unicorns, and rainbows, no more war or suffering due to divisiveness and competition, conceptually. In that case, it can feel like freedom, especially the endgame. But to get there, that feels daunting. Can we do it one person at a time? How many people are on Earth to date? And how low on the scale of emotions, or in the frequency of energy, does all of this either/or land?

Yes, I am very aware. That rant is based on the perception that we are victims of circumstance rather than in control of whatever we create in our circumstances and experiences. I realize that good and bad is how we have defined most behavior and many people. My career was spent in the prison system, specifically supporting people who made "bad" choices. And more specifically, people who made bad choices related to substance use. I grew up indoctrinated in a belief system of good and bad, heaven and hell, and in a family stricken with a condition called "I-can't-be-wrong-itis."

Considering I am in the infancy of expanding my perception, awakening, or remembering, I will choose to be patient with integrating this concept of everything being *and,* and *both,* and the gifts it has to offer. I do acknowledge that my parents taught what they were taught, what the generations before believed was the right thing. I have moved past feeling victimized or duped by the beliefs of others. I understand that no one did anything to me with nefarious intentions. My resistance to religious beliefs has lost its *oomph!* so to speak. At this stage in the game, I choose otherwise and can leave it at that—for today anyway. I maintain that harm continues to be inflicted around the world in the name of religion, but that is just another indication of what the guides describe: The perpetuation of suffering caused by division, separation, and the belief that someone must be right and someone wrong.

As Emily Fletcher stated at a recent Gaia Emersion Conference, "Heaven is not a destination; it is a frequency." So, as we have seen in other Active Connections, if energy is everything and everything is energy, *we consciousness* is us remembering that, integrating that, embodying that, and connecting with the nonphysical from a higher frequency state, the same nonphysical that is a part of us and that we are a part of.

So, yes, I am a work (and play) in progress. I have yet to meet a breathing human who is not. I find it uncomfortable being around people who are contrary, argumentative, and who must be right. As

I read that back, I smiled because I still do have an insatiable desire to be right. And some say we resist or judge in others what we see and resist in ourselves, which can feel crappy and humbling. But I choose, when possible, not to be around others in that energy frequency. I choose to be around like-minded and like-hearted people and in environments that are easy and enjoyable for my own energy frequency's sake. And when I am not, how can I help others raise their frequency, even in small ways, and maintain that higher vibration in any environment?

I have much to learn and room to grow and expand always and in all ways. Most importantly, though, I am choosing to enjoy this adventure while living my Divine Intent within a fulfilling, purposeful life that potentially makes a difference in the lives of others. It is a conscious, high frequency decision each day, through my thoughts and emotions, through my writing, my relationships, and my interactions with everyone I meet.

So, to wrap up on a more positive note, a frequency of hope, suspend the *how* of it for a moment, and imagine the world as the guides describe the *we consciousness* and the new paradigm. See and feel a world of connection, support, peace, community, compassion, inclusivity, nonduality, and breathe in the harmony and loveliness of that. Imagine we are all a part of one energy source, all streams of that energy of pure oneness, all experiencing heaven on Earth.

Vince and Mary's Reflections

The topic of this session is challenging to accept. Most of childhood is spent with someone in charge or an authority figure telling, teaching, or lecturing us on what was right and what was wrong. It takes trust to accept that even our science tells us there is no right or wrong. I definitely see how the either/or world that we have created and chosen to live in has caused so many conflicts and wars. The question is, can we accept this concept and allow others to have their beliefs and truths? Can we be right in our own minds without needing to make someone else wrong? Can we admit someone else is right without making ourselves wrong?

We love that Michele shares that this concept is almost too abstract to comprehend, and that is only the case because of what we have been taught. And if we admit it, we agree to it without even challenging the concept. We blindly accept that it is either this or that. As she went on to share, we are concerned that we might not be able to navigate life if we don't know what is right or wrong. Guidance didn't share that we can't stand for something. They shared that just because we stand for it doesn't mean anyone else has to. And if they don't, it doesn't make them wrong.

Choosing to live from an either/or viewpoint creates the opportunity for judgment. And judgment leads to separation, both internally and externally. Living from a both/and viewpoint doesn't say you agree with the other person. It says you are willing to allow them to have their way just as you have your way. When you allow others, and they allow you, every creation and co-creation can be used fully.

The need to be right comes from our underlying need to be worthy. We have proven our worth by doing the right thing, knowing the right answer, and unfortunately many times by making others wrong. In a Universe based on love, how can there be right or wrong, either/or? The challenge is trusting enough to reframe the old belief.

Introspective Insights:

(Take a few minutes to journal or meditate on the following questions.)

1. What areas of your life are most affected by living an either/or existence?
2. Where would you rather be unhappy or all alone than be wrong?
3. What specific circumstances would cause you to find it hard to accept there is no right or wrong?
4. How would your life be different if this concept were true?

Gratitude
(AC 23 Nov 23)

The cycles of evolution have been experienced throughout the eons and throughout every corner of the universe. The stages are well known and all of you on Earth at this time chose to be, during this stage. The movement from "I" to "we" is in progress. You wanted to be part of this transformation.

The Round Table, channeled by Vince Kramer

You have shared about stepping into life and honoring this time in our country with appreciation and gratitude. Can you share about the country and world in this now, where there should be appreciation and gratitude?

> Yes, we will. Let's look at things from the individual level. There is no one living in the third- or fourth-dimension worlds that energetically didn't make the choice to be in the experience that they are in, each choosing a journey on their planet to expand the energy of the whole.
>
> As you share, that choice includes agreements, circumstances, people, etc., to fully live the life they chose to live to accomplish

that purpose. This means that, as individuals and as a collective, everything in your lives is valuable and necessary to your journey. As you learn to believe in this understanding of your experience, you will learn that what you call the new paradigm is nothing more than what it is.

Each person who co-creates with you is a reason for appreciation and gratitude. Each circumstance that you experience is a reason for appreciation and gratitude. Every emotion you experience is a message to who you are choosing to be in that moment and is a reason for appreciation and gratitude.

Be especially thankful for what causes the greatest challenges, for they are the biggest gifts. Each gift you create or co-create in your life brings you closer to sharing your light, unobstructed, out into the world, and closer to being that expansive force expanding the source energy. Each one supports you in living your 3D Divine Intent and helping others fully live theirs.

As a country, your United States is collectively creating and co-creating everything that will assist you all in no longer accepting the duality and separateness that has been a large part of your history and has, over time, become even more aligned with the devastation and destruction of each person for themselves.

Be grateful for all of these co-creations and creations. They will support you all in moving into the paradigm of unity. Appreciate and have gratitude as the outside observations mirror to you the separation that is in your community, your family, and most importantly, inside of you. Then, use the vibration of your appreciation and gratitude to heal the self-chosen wounds created by the separation in you and, in turn, the separation in your family, community, country, and world. Be grateful for each step of the journey to oneness.

In this now, Namaste.

Michele's Musings

So, in my mind, this is what they seem to be saying: It is not only the good things that happen to us (or for us) that are reasons to feel grateful—the supportive and kind people in our lives, the money we make, the healthy, able bodies we have, our food, or the adventures we take—but also that we chose it all, including the not-so-good, and all of it is still reason to be grateful and appreciative.

I find it challenging to appreciate a recent diagnosis of polymyalgia rheumatica or to be grateful for the pain I am in daily (and nightly) due to this autoimmune condition. I had never heard of it until I was the recipient of it. The guides explain that every emotion communicates who we are choosing to be moment to moment, but there are mornings I wake up feeling frustrated and tired, another disrupted sleep caused by pain in my shoulders, hips, spine, and neck. Am I choosing or causing the condition? Did I plan it before birth as something to experience this time around? Or does that matter, and am I really, at each moment, just choosing the negative (low frequency) response to it? Can I transform the emotional state of frustration into a healing state of gratitude and appreciation, and will my body get the memo? And would I then just be bypassing and not processing the unpleasant but real feelings?

I recognize that on the emotional scale, I am starting the day in frustration or sometimes lower, disappointment, and even lower, anger. These are halfway down the scale and further. Joy, appreciation, empowerment, freedom, and love are at the top, and fear, grief, desperation, despair, and powerlessness are at the bottom. This means my energetic frequency could use a boost. Since we can only be in one emotional state at a time, frustration, for example, I would have to avoid spiraling to even lower frequency emotions as the day unfolded if a higher one was the goal.

During the Take a Quantum Leap program, I became aware of my responsibility and my choice of where my energy is every day. I can choose to stay in frustration and possibly move down the scale to feeling angry and even crappier by telling myself the following: "OMG! I hate this pain! I'm so tired! I'm so sick of not getting a good night's sleep! I hate my body! This sucks so bad!" Those thoughts would take me further down the scale and a world away from gratitude and appreciation. How could I be grateful and feel joy in that state? I could not.

What I learned was that I could change the thoughts to even just a little higher up the scale, to maybe some "what ifs." What if this was a wake-up call to listen to my body, to change some beliefs about raising my energetic frequency to one of self-care and healing, to say no when necessary, and even at some point to accept and love my body? What if I had planned this before I was born for a reason that is not clear yet? Maybe I had something to learn about changing my thoughts and emotions and transforming how I live my day-to-day life, knowing I am in control of how I feel. And within the illness, is there any space at all for feeling grateful? I guess now I can give myself permission to rest any time during my days; that was never a thing before, and I am learning how to better take care of my physical body through this experience. It is also an *every-present-moment* opportunity to practice raising my frequency, which is not always easy. I am finding, though, that I appreciate the loving support I have through it.

And yes, I know it is ridiculous to say "Abracadabra! Now I shall feel joy and appreciation!" Bypassing natural feelings and emotions causes more problems because none of it is real. Faking it is avoiding it, and, worse, storing it in our bodies. If you have ever been around someone who is "pretend positive," it is exasperating! In the new paradigm I can feel what I feel, but now I decide how long to remain in that state. And I know how to transform my state. What are some easy, quick steps that do not directly involve the process of changing our thoughts but will boost our emotional state? For me, I love the smell of essential oils; I love being in nature; I love having a soak in the bathtub; I love a fresh cup of coffee in the morning or a walk with loved ones. These all raise my energetic vibration to a higher frequency.

At any time, though, I can directly change my thoughts, preferably sooner rather than later to lessen the suffering caused by them. I can recognize where my emotions are, then the beliefs underlying the thoughts that landed me there.

Sometimes, it is easier to understand the high frequency energy of thoughts and emotions, such as gratitude and appreciation, when we see the contrasting thoughts and emotions. Before I retired a few years ago, I had read about how our thoughts affect our emotions, and so for one day, I decided to experiment, to write whatever thoughts popped into my head.

(Please forgive the expletives, and trust that since that time and loads of learning and growing, I have softened my language and critical self-judgment considerably.)

"OMG, I look tired!"

"Shit! I shouldn't have weighed myself!" "I'm so fucking fat!"

"I hate mornings!"

"Holy crap, I look old!"

"Shit! I don't want to go to work!"

"I'm so fucking tired!"

"I hate my job!"

"Wow, that was a stupid thing to say to him!"

"I look horrible!"

"What the hell happened to my neck? It's wrinkled, so gross!"

"I should've known better!"

"What are they thinking about me?"

"That was a stupid thing to do!"

"OMG! I'm a horrible person!"

"I look sick, so ugly!"

And all this before noon.

Now, contrast those with the following: I am so grateful for another day. I appreciate that I had a great career. I am grateful for my partner, for our walks, for my family, for my friends, for my home, and for being surrounded by nature. I am grateful for the good work that I did to support others and how I continue to be a source of support for myself and others.

Sometimes, the awareness of my thoughts comes first, then the resulting emotions, and other times, it is the loud and clear supercharged emotions that instantly lead the way. It sounds like the chicken and the egg scenario, but ultimately, the thoughts come first, whether I am aware of them or not. The thoughts cause and supersede the emotional reaction, and the foundation of the thought is a belief. I understand it because I have been practicing it. For my medical condition, "I did something to cause the condition." Or "I must've deserved this," or "I'll never be able to fix it, and neither will the doctors." "I'm just going to get worse." "I hate my body!"

The formula, as I understand it so far, is that beliefs create thoughts, thoughts create emotions, and then I choose the action to take. Thoughts can also create beliefs because, as we mentioned previously, beliefs are just thoughts we think over and over, and around and around we go. And it is all up to me. I am at the wheel. I create a higher energetic frequency or a lower one. I feel better or worse; I decide. Sounds easy, but it is not. It is raising the level of how conscious I am as I move about my day (or night). And I continue to work at it because I like to feel better and suffer less on purpose. Life is too short, as they say.

Recently, I realized the fear I had surrounding gratitude and appreciation. It is a weird one, one that I did not notice or name before, but it was simmering below the surface for possibly decades. What if I create and co-create the amazing things I have always wanted, just for it all to be taken away or not to last? "Don't appreciate it too much; before you know it, it'll be gone!" What a horrible belief! And sort of a protective one, because it protects me from the disappointment of losing whatever I wanted and received, especially if I would just stop wanting and receiving. It is the voice of my subpersonalities, of course, ever the protectors but also the interferers. Imagine creating a life you want and love, only to expend much energy worrying and feeling fearful that it will not last or will be taken away. Where the hell did that belief come from? And how low is that energetic frequency?

Now imagine a default emotional state, vibrating at a high energetic frequency, creating and co-creating the life you imagined, feeling free and empowered in knowing how to raise your frequency even when the shite hits the fan. Our beliefs and thoughts cause a drop into doubt, worry, jealousy, blame, or worse. And imagine the freedom and empowerment that all the possibilities are ours for the choosing, and that there exists only choices: no victims, mistakes, or coincidences. Some of it still feels like a stretch to me, especially the "biggest challenges are our biggest gifts" part. Still, with practice in raising my level of awareness (or consciousness) related to my beliefs, thoughts, and emotions, all of what I planned to experience in this lifetime will eventually and naturally transform into reasons of appreciation and gratitude. Yes, as the guides explain, even the gifts that may not feel like gifts at the time.

The hope in the Active Connection is that we are changing, no longer accepting separateness and duality, and that the creation and co-creation in the United States indicate and cause this transformation. We perceive this chaos as a gift worth feeling grateful for because we are moving toward the new paradigm that is on the other side of divisiveness and separateness.

Every emotion we experience is a message of who we are choosing to be in that moment, in every moment, and that is a reason for appreciation and gratitude. And when I am not in the mood for gratitude or appreciation, I see my granddaughters in my mind's eye. Done. I see the birds in the bird feeder just outside the window. Done. I see the sun shining on the lake. Done. I close my eyes and breathe in the cool, crisp spring air. Done.

Vince and Mary's Reflections

The power of this guidance is in its simplicity and directness. There is nothing in our lives that didn't happen because of us. Most importantly, everything that has happened in our lives has been for us. Each is an orchestrated harmony of our creations and co-creations with others to best serve us in living the life we are meant to live.

They adamantly shared that everything is on purpose. We like the fact that they shared that we bring agreements into this lifetime to help us fully expand into who we are meant to be. These agreements are for us and others on our respective journeys.

It was extremely empowering for us to learn that there is a gift in every circumstance and situation in our lives. It removed the belief or misconception that we are victims of the world around us. And even more exciting, when you find a gift in a tragedy of the past, you rewrite your history.

We find it empowering that every person we interact with is sharing a better understanding of who we are, just by being who they are. And... we do the same for them. It is easy to see what quantum physics tells us. There are no mistakes or coincidences.

It is exciting to realize that the greatest challenges in our lives bring us the greatest gifts. It is empowering to know that we actually become more of who we are and are meant to be. This realization makes me want to encourage more challenges and gives me the courage to face them for what they truly are.

We certainly understand Michele's perspective when she talks about trying to find a gift in her diagnosis. Our pain, displeasure, and sometimes fear make it extremely difficult to even consider there could be a gift. When our bodies are in pain, or our hearts broken, we are blinded to new paradigm thoughts.

Michele points out something crucial to understand when she says that we can't be in high and low vibrations at the same time. She also shares a valuable understanding when she talks about moving up the vibrational scale in steps. It is challenging to move all the way up the scale. A bite at a time can make the move into your highest vibration easier.

We also want to recognize Michele's vulnerability in sharing her fears and doubts. These concepts aren't difficult, but they are new, and they take time. Also, we have to have compassion because the concepts are so different from the collective energy. Different means change, and change can be difficult, especially when there is little support around you.

The empowering thing about all of this, it is happening for you and because of you. Each instance, new understanding, and gift is another opportunity for gratitude. The highest vibration.

Introspective Insights:
(Take a few minutes to journal or meditate on the following questions.)

1. Where have there been times in your life when you have felt you were a victim?
2. Can you find a gift in each of those situations?
3. Where can you show more gratitude in and for your life?
4. What have you gained or learned from the biggest challenges in your life?

Supporting the Children
(AC 22 Dec 23)

After choosing your reason for incarnating on the Earth plane as a strand of universal energy, you chose your parents and grandparents to help you learn and experience the circumstances and develop the beliefs that will help you become all you are meant to be to live the reason you chose fully.

The Round Table, channeled by Vince Kramer

Can you share about our time with grandchildren and children?

> We are happy to share the importance of the time you have with them. The importance comes no matter your level of consciousness or understanding of your effect on them.
>
> Every parent and grandparent knows they are responsible for helping the young grow up in your 3D world. But few know the importance of supporting them in remembering what they know. And nurturing them in finding their own way.
>
> It is your job as a parent or grandparent to help the young ones stay safe as they find their way and develop everything they need to help them uncover the gifts and talents that will help them in living their reason for being.

Adults must realize that children are still very connected and remember who they truly are. If that remembering is supported and help is given to continue this knowing, you will help them stay connected to the support you all have in every dimension.

Can you share more about what we remember at a young age?

It depends on the energy of the child and the Divine Intent chosen. Each and every one of you has your own individual journey and paths you can take. The circumstances and people you choose determine the experience of remembering or forgetting, connecting or losing the connection, and things like seeing energies and traveling through dimensions.

For the parents and grandparents who know these energetic concepts and have been reacquainted with a level of understanding of the oneness of all, it is the reason that the new human chose you to help them on their journey. It was a choice to have you to help them not forget or remember when they do. As you awaken more and understand your own connection to source energy, you can choose to support them even more. It was your choice to help them not forget. You were chosen by them because you were willing to help.

You can choose to use what you know and understand to support them and to believe that will move them through their chosen journey and in living their chosen Divine Intent faster. There will be many opportunities to give them assistance in all aspects of their experience based on your knowing that it must be their way and that you are here to help them find it and live it.

Sometimes, it may be showing them a new way. Other times, it might be just neutralizing the effects of those who have not awakened or chosen to live from a new paradigm.

Keep sharing, keep loving, keep being yourselves as examples of love and willingness. Shine the light of who you each are.

In this now, Namaste.

Michele's Musings

I was flying home to Canada from a retreat in Mount Shasta, California, in October 2023. I was between flights in the Seattle airport when my daughter called. I could hear the stress in her voice, and I knew something had happened at home. My daughter said she was taking her daughter to the emergency room because something was seriously wrong.

A brief backstory: My granddaughter had experienced anxiety at the start of the school year, usually showing up as stomach pain, tears, and a call to pick her up from school. She had been struggling with the classroom environment since September, and although she was academically doing well (for grade two), she had difficulty when students were acting out, when noise levels were heightened, and especially at times when the principal would remove a student physically. My daughter had provided her with professional support, and the teachers had been trying their best to be helpful.

My granddaughter was six years old at this time, and I knew since she was around three that she communicated regularly with her invisible friend Sophia. Many kids had invisible friends, so it did not seem strange. She spoke of Sophia like she was with her physically. When my granddaughter was with me and having a conversation with Sophia, I just enjoyed that she was tapped into her imagination and maybe her intuition. How cool for a three-year-old! Early last October, before I left for Mount Shasta, my daughter called to ask about something strange happening with her daughter. My daughter described how my granddaughter stated she could look down and see her body in bed as she fell asleep. And how she loved traveling to places in her sleep, whenever and wherever she wanted to go. She shared that Care Bear Land, with the rainbows made of candy, was her favorite place. I explained that she was doing something called *astral projection* and that I had taken a course about it on Vancouver Island. I explained that her daughter was also lucid dreaming, and I had taken courses and read numerous books on that ability. My daughter was exasperated and a bit confused, but at least she had some answers, even if they sounded weird to her.

A week later, late at night in the Seattle airport, my daughter was on the phone, frustrated, not knowing what to do with her daughter who was screaming under her bed because she wanted the "people" to stop bothering her. How awful for this little girl and for her mom, not knowing what was happening or how to stop it. For my daughter, through her professional lens as a registered nurse, the logical thing was to take her to the emergency room, and this was above my metaphysical pay grade. I had learned a lot of things in the past of the woo-woo world, but this hit too close to home, and I knew one thing for certain: I did not want this little one medicated out of what she was experiencing. On the other hand, I also did not want her to be suffering and feeling helpless.

So, at six years old, she had been connecting with her guide, Sophia, for at least three years. More recently, she articulated experiences of astral travel and lucid dreaming and was talking to the non-physical energy of people who had died. I was in the Seattle airport asking my daughter to hold off on the emergency room visit and explaining that this may not be a psychotic episode or any other serious mental health crisis. I shared a plan, a way that we could first consider that there might be something else happening. If my idea worked, we could rule out a mental health crisis; if it did not work, then appropriate medical assistance would be sought.

I messaged a local person, a widow, a mom of three boys whose husband died in a farm accident a few years prior. Her story was tragic and extraordinary. She experienced unusual regular connections with her deceased husband; they conversed as if he was in the physical state. After researching what was happening to her (she was new to the world of nonphysical connection), she was drawn to learning about and completing training in sound healing. Her intuitive abilities were awakened after her husband died. Her modality was sound healing, which connects to the consciousness and the subconsciousness to assess what is occurring and what is needed to release and heal using tuning forks/sound frequency to balance the energetic frequency and align the energy centers.

I took my granddaughter the following day. The practitioner helped her understand what was happening, to know she was safe, and that she had special gifts like the practitioner's. She also explained to my daughter what was happening and how she could help her daughter feel safe and empowered to control the experiences, especially when she wanted to sleep at night without being bothered by nonphysical beings.

On the drive to the session that day, my granddaughter told me that Sophia spoke to her in a different language and that Sophia was teaching her that same language, which was a mixture between French and Japanese. How interesting that at her young age, she was talking about *light language*, and even more extraordinary, referring to two languages that she had never heard. I was vaguely familiar with high frequency light language, and I shared how cool it was that she was learning. Hearing about these experiences articulated in her small child language made all of it more real than ever in my life. It is one thing to dabble in all sorts of interesting phenomena and quite another to have it solidified through a young child, especially a precious grandchild.

This Active Connection resonated in an exceptional way because of this recent revelation. My job is to assist in a nurturing and supportive way as they both find their unique way of processing everything that is occurring and will most likely continue to occur.

At one point, my daughter said, "I wish it would all just go away. I can't stand to see her terrified!" She also wanted to know the point of it all, the endgame. I explained my understanding at the time, that her daughter would have the ability not only to connect to her intuition, her gut sense, her innate wisdom, but also to trust it, that she would know who to choose as friends and partners, and that she would continue to connect with Sophia, a part of her own inner guidance and discern how to maneuver in her life. She would trust her guidance, teach others, and help in extraordinary ways. I felt honored to assist in the ways the guides shared through Vince. I choose consciously to help her *not* forget when conversations are prompted by her. The new paradigm is about being committed to sharing, to being myself, and to being an example of love and willingness for my granddaughters and anyone connecting with an open and willing heart.

As per Vince's question, can you share more about what you remember from a young age? It will be interesting to watch my granddaughters grow, see the paths they choose, and see the Divine Intent each had planned and how they choose to live it fully. Will they remember who they are or why they chose to be here? Will they remain open to my understanding and support? Will they choose to live in a new paradigm way, living their purpose, their Divine Intent, connecting to guidance in the highest frequencies of their energy streams? That continues to be my love-infused hope for them.

Vince and Mary's Reflections

As guidance shared in the Active Connection session, the role of parent and grandparent is much different from what has been believed in the past. This guidance that has been readily available to all of us all along isn't bad or scary. It can be confusing and concerning to a young child and parents who have been taught or came to believe that only crazy people hear voices. It is a challenge for us as grown-ups to look at our beliefs and ask if they are really true or just something that has been limiting us.

Michele chose to open her mind to new possibilities and support not just her granddaughter but also her daughter. She supported her granddaughter by not making her wrong. She supported her daughter in presenting a new way of thinking beyond what she taught her as a child. As will be presented in the Active Connection guidance throughout this book, we all have the ability to tap into the knowledge of the Universe. We are only limited by the limiting beliefs we have chosen to accept from others, and we can choose new beliefs at any time. In the meantime, be aware of the beliefs you are sharing with your children and grandchildren. Support them in finding their way. Allow them to pursue all possibilities and keep them physically safe along the way.

Introspective Insights:

(Take a few minutes to journal or meditate on the following questions.)

1. Where have you shut out your guidance?
2. What beliefs that limit you have you been sharing with the young people in your life?
3. How can you help your children or grandchildren not forget what they obviously remember?
4. How can you help them develop beliefs that support and empower them?

Next Steps
(AC 23 Feb 24)

You are being called to so much more and to see and understand the opportunities in front of you, you must be ready to raise your level of awareness, your level of consciousness. There is a new paradigm ready for you to step into. Only you can choose to follow what is presenting itself to you.

The Round Table, channeled by Vince Kramer

Sometimes, I'm unsure what questions to ask. What are some of the things we haven't talked about that are important for us to know and understand?

> There is so much that is already in front of you and to come in the movement into a new paradigm and a new way of being. Let's talk about the things that are and have been in front of you. There are many beliefs you hold that have been handed down from generation to generation. There are also beliefs that society or the collective holds that most of you hold that would be helpful to understand at a higher vibrational level.
>
> Things like energetics and the actual processes that you all go through from the time you chose to experience the third dimen-

sion until the time you answered the calling to awaken to all of who you are and can be on the planet of your choice. Some examples are your soul agreements, creating circumstances that are very important opportunities for you on your journey to live your journey, and your Unique Purpose on the Earth plane.

It goes beyond beliefs. There is much for you to learn about how you can break the cycle and support those energy streams that have chosen you to provide guidance and help them on their chosen journeys. You can support them and help them navigate the journey faster and maybe even more easily than your experience.

Some things are necessary to know and understand so you can move beyond those barriers or blockages that have kept you the same, not necessarily because you don't want to transform, but mostly because you don't know that you can transform. The second area where more information will assist you in living more fully the life you are meant to live, is in learning about implementing in your own lives the concepts of the new paradigm. There are many opportunities for you in the unknown, and learning how to discover, create, and live the life you are meant to live will help you not only recognize these opportunities but also how to create and manifest them into your lives.

There are concepts beyond what the masses accept that will support you in stepping more fully into who you truly are as an energy. They will rocket you into living a life that brings you great joy and satisfaction, a life where abundance flows to you freely.

There is much to know and understand about creation and co-creation. We would love to talk with you more about energy, living on purpose, being all that you can be, oneness and unity, community, transformation, and self-empowerment. There is much to share that will help you step more fully and with ease into a higher level of consciousness, a new awareness that will support you in being all that you are meant to be, having all that you are meant to have, and doing all that you are meant to do. As we share these concepts with you and help you understand them, the Universe will expand, and there will be more to learn and share because of the expansion. Your new level of consciousness and awareness will open the door to new unknowns and opportunities to be more of you and to help others do the same.

Know that we are always here for you to guide, share, and help you live this life you chose as fully as possible. We are here to support you in living your Divine Intent, your reason for being. All you have to do is ask the questions. By asking, you are giving us permission to give you more, let you know how to get unstuck, and to be all that you can be. Your journey is our journey, and we are ecstatic to be on it with you.

In this now, Namaste.

Michele's Musings

There are not many people in my neck of the woods (yes, I am aware no one says "neck of the woods" anymore) who I would feel comfortable discussing soul agreements with. It is unfortunate because I love learning about soul agreements. Maybe that will change in the not-too-distant future, especially with the new paradigm unfolding. I feel it in the air! Now, how can we gently help others understand what this is and then help each other maneuver through the transformation of experiencing a natural state of higher frequency energy, community, and oneness? I am ready to learn more.

So, next steps… hmm, I like that. It means that we have accomplished something and are advancing. What are the concepts of this new paradigm, and how do we implement them in our lives? My life is relatively simple. I live simply and decluttered. My responsibilities are few: I am retired, doing the things I love to do, spending time with people I enjoy spending time with, learning and expanding my knowledge, and creating through writing.

I am aware of the vulnerability of this creative endeavor, but at the same time, it is not about me—and it is all about me, about

EVERYONE. I will be fully and transparently out of hiding. The concepts of the new paradigm are for everyone, but inclusivity does not necessarily mean openness, receptivity, or acceptance for the masses. The concepts will not be palatable or interesting to everyone because we are living different human lives, and we are all over the map, with everyone on different paths. Now, when I expand that lens and perceive our connectedness to each other, with the spider web of energy connected to and streaming from the main energy generator, I can understand what "next steps" mean in this context.

Based on my limited but expanding understanding, it is not about convincing anyone or being right or wrong. It is about setting out a delicious five-course meal with a lovely invitation to partake and expand the palate, as one chooses to accept, or not. I have yet to meet someone with a perfectly blissful life. Even the *Real Housewives of Beverly Hills,* that I may or may not admit to watching, have an abundance of cash but lack satisfaction and joy, or it is just all a scripted and somewhat entertaining mess. Either way, the new paradigm is about finding contentment, purpose, satisfaction, co-creation, and great joy, no matter the societal status. Ironically, though, this shift potentially boosts abundance in every aspect of our lives if we are open and allow it.

I look forward to further expanding into a new level of consciousness and awareness and to experiencing true liberation from disempowering belief systems at long last. The enthusiasm and openness are a start. I have much to learn, and I deeply appreciate the time to do so. It starts with me, decluttering more than my living space. What precious gems will be discovered as I continue to challenge the beliefs and upgrade my energetic frequency daily with aligned, empowering thoughts and upscale emotions? And with all the support and inner guidance constantly and conveniently—much less than a stone's throw away—all within us.

Thankfully, the new paradigm and its concepts will continue to unfold as this co-creative endeavor evolves and expands. Along with that, I have the anticipation of participating wholeheartedly and transforming with ease, joy, and loving unity.

Vince and Mary's Reflections

This guidance helped us better understand what it will take to move into the new paradigm. It highlighted the journey in very basic terms and, at the same time, gave us something we can rely on as we awaken. The cycle of the past has kept us the same, but it is empowering to know we are meant to take it forward. By learning more, we can take the next step. This is truly a project we have set out on. We are learning as we go!! It was encouraging knowing the transformation has been slow, not because we resist, but because we aren't sure how. Knowing that we can get the *hows* and *whys* through these sessions is encouraging and that guidance is more than willing to share it is even more encouraging.

For some reason, I don't think the new paradigm is about comfort. Just by using the adjective "new," comfort seems challenged. One of our favorite reminders from guidance over the years has been that the life we are meant to live, the life we each chose, is in the unknown. We have never been there before. The "unknown" itself brings discomfort. It is a discomfort that we all must step through to live the reason we came to Earth. It really means we must be willing to live a new way. That is uncomfortable for all of us.

When Michele shares that we are all on different paths, it is so true. But the paths are more the same than they are different. The path that each of us is on is one of awakening to and living the life we chose before we were even born. The path is taking us to the new paradigm. We are all on different parts of that path, though. Some are further down the path, and others are not so far. No matter if it is because of natural progression or resistance, everyone will be asked or prodded to wake up and step into the new paradigm.

Introspective Insights:
(Take a few minutes to journal or meditate on the following questions.)

1. Where have you chosen to step into a higher level of awareness?
2. What fears do you have around a new paradigm that is about living your life your way?
3. What are the precious gems in your life that have been buried in the muck of old beliefs?
4. What would life be like if you willingly stepped into the new paradigm?

Death
(AC 8 Jan 24)

You are on the Earth plane to fully live your chosen reason for being to expand Universal Energy. When you complete this mission, you will once again enfold into the fullness of the vibration of not just the energy streams you represent but into the fullness and all the glory of Universal Energy.

The Round Table, channeled by Vince Kramer

Could you share with us what happens after death for us?

It would be an honor to help you all understand the experience of death and what happens after it.

First, remember that you are all multidimensional beings, and your experience is always on multiple planes of existence. You have heard the phrase, "You are spiritual beings having an earthly experience." We would like to take that further by saying that you are an energetic being. You are on Earth to expand your energy stream and to live the Divine Intent you, as an energy stream, chose for your time on Earth.

When the time comes in your life, where through choice you have accomplished what you will accomplish in your earthly experience, you will start the process of leaving the earthly plane and return to the higher vibration of your energy stream.

What is that like for us?

It can and will be different for each person, just like everything that happens in the third dimension. It is a creation or co-creation. For some, it may be quick and easy, like in a car accident. For others, it may be quiet and uneventful, like transitioning in your sleep. For others, it could be a violent death, a co-creation of a murder, or a shooting spree. And yet for others, a lingering death in a hospital room or a hospice bed.

No matter the way, it is a creation or a co-creation. Your Higher Self, that nonphysical part of your choosing a creation to help you live your reason for being on Earth right up to your last breath.

What about the body and the resistance to dying that seems to happen for many?

Know that it is all part of the co-creation, but also remember that the body is operated by the subconscious or unconsciously. This means that it is programmed to function. It also means that it is greatly affected by your subpersonalities. They can take over and refuse to die until the body can no longer exist. At that time, they no longer resist.

You say each death is a creation or co-creation. Can you share more about this concept?

Yes, each circumstance is a created opportunity—the nonphysical, all-knowing part of you helping you fulfill your reason for the trip to this planet. It will always be to help you fully live or as fully as humanly possible to live your Divine Intent, your reason for being—each co-creation in its own purpose. Let us give you some examples.

A lingering death may be the perfect opportunity to help loved ones come to terms with or understand past interactions that have disempowered them and help them find a new understanding. It also can be an opportunity to see and interact one more time with someone who needs closure. A quick, violent death could be a co-creation with society as a whole to help see a situation or a growing problem that must be addressed in society like duality, homelessness, and lack of respect for life. Just know that there truly are no mistakes or coincidences.

There is some opportunity for growth and expansion in every creation and co-creation, even in death. The transition is enfolding back into the full magnificence of the dying person's energy stream. It is a return to all-knowingness and high vibration. It is returning to all there is in your part in the wholeness of the Universe, and all there is.

In this now and every now, know that all is created and co-created for and by you. Namaste.

Michele's Musings

It was Christmas Eve; the hospital room was at capacity with the family gathered around Dad. Unintentionally, our breathing synchronized with his slow breaths. We knew it was close.

A few days prior, feeling jet lagged from a brief, warm getaway, I returned to work on a frigid morning with a busy day ahead, including a staff meeting and Christmas luncheon I was responsible for managing. My phone rang. It was one of my brothers. Dad had days or maybe hours to live. His organs were shutting down. He was a healthy, active eighty-three-year-old, still golfing, working summers at the golf course, and curling and bowling in the off-season. He had just had the flu before we left for Mexico. It did not make sense!

It was almost time for my staff meeting to start. I had thought I could get through the few hours and then leave for the hospital ninety minutes away, but I could not move. I could not think. I started to cry. I did not think I could compose myself long enough to chair the meeting, and I did not feel like celebrating the holidays with my employees.

When I arrived at the hospital, Dad was tired but still able to talk, so I was grateful to spend time with him. I was in his room when the physician shared the grim news. Dad listened quietly, nodded that yes, he understood, and bravely said he knew what was next.

After the doctor left, Dad reinforced to me and my brother that he did not want any exceptional measures to prolong his life. He was ready. He shared his wishes for his funeral. Dad was clear and calm. I felt my insides collapsing. I was in shock. This was it.

Gratefully, Dad was able to visit with us and, in tune with his usual demeanor, said things that made us all laugh. His sense of humor never left him until his voice left him the last day.

Each Christmas Eve since then, we honor our dad by connecting with each other, acknowledging and remembering the ever-present imprint of his beautiful, loving energy on our hearts. Did he preplan how he would leave this physical existence? Did we co-create it this way, so we could all have time to say goodbye? Guidance in the Active Connection were a soothing balm, even after seven years. What did we all gain from this death experience? It was interesting how the last of six brothers who had flown across countries arrived just as Dad was taking his last breath. I hear of that occurring often.

I had never lost someone this close. I had never been with anyone as they died. It was heart-wrenching and beautifully woven together. Dad was loved so much, and all that love could not change the inevitable; rather, it somehow infused the sadness with such peace. It is clear that he fulfilled his purpose for that lifetime. His memory continues to inspire me to live a life infused with love, with integrity, and consciously enjoying each day as it unfolds. In his memory, I am open to the possibilities that invite me to live my life as fully as possible before dying, just as I had planned before arriving.

The experience of losing my dad came to mind as I listened to this Active Connection about death. My experience of loss is limited, but I think about the potential loss of loved ones with more dread than is probably healthy, so I was interested in the guide's explanation. Death can be such a tricky concept; it is inevitable and expected, and there is an understandable acute fragility about it, especially in the culture within which I live. Some cultures view death with varying degrees of dread or obsession. I remember gasping when I first heard the nonphysical energy of Abraham through Esther Hicks, referring to people who died as "croaked." How could they be so nonchalant about something so somber, serious, dreaded, and tragic? Strangely, the more I heard it called croaking, a deeper part of me felt some relief. I did not understand why at the time.

Some cultures see the physical body as just a husk of the true self, so seeing dead bodies is not perceived with the same horror because they understand the body is not their loved one. How freeing would that be? Would it be possible for us to see death differently? Could we grieve as naturally needed (whatever that is) and eventually return to living a full, content life, holding our loved ones in our memories but with lighter emotions attached? That sounds a bit stoic and ironic, especially as I confess that it took more than a few months to feel like myself again after losing my beloved fourteen-year-old Lhasa apso, Cooper. I struggled to be alone in the house; the grief felt like a sludgy abyss that would surely overtake me. I missed him so much because I was with him, cared for him, and snuggled him every day. The sadness visited for longer than I would have expected. In fact, it moved in with me. To make things more challenging, we tend to suffer alone in this type of grief. It is not viewed as "appropriate grief" by pet-less people. They do not understand, so compassion is not as free flowing, unfortunately.

The Active Connection offers a softer way to view death (if we can consider such a thing). The guides describe different ways humans *choose* to leave their physical state, the beneficial reasons to them and loved ones, and why we might choose from an assortment of ways. A question surfaced: What was the benefit of a relative or her bereaved family when she died at thirty-six years old? That one continues to evade me.

I do not want to die, and even more, I do not want to lose anyone else close to me. I am sure I am not alone with this grasping, as the Buddhists would say. I am hoping (in a gritted teeth sort of way) that before I was born, I chose a relatively quick way so I could say goodbye and do so with little or no pain.

So, I am curious about a few things related to death. Do we get stronger or more resilient the more we experience loss, or does it get easier the older we get? Do we suffer less grief-wise if we grow up in a culture that views death as a natural transition rather than an absolute end? I have not yet experienced loss to the extent of many others in my circle of friends and family. Still, recently, I experienced a prolonged visceral *nearing my own death* experience.

For six months, I woke up abruptly during the night, almost every night, in a terrified state of fear. My thoughts... *I am dying! It must be my heart! I feel like I'm dying! OMG, I'm alone! When will they find my body? And who will finally find it? What the hell?!!*

Something felt terribly wrong physically. And worse, I was alone. My husband was working away for six months, so as excited as I was to have some *me* time, my subconscious freaked out! And he was only an hour away! I could visit whenever I wanted to, but that choice was not one of comfort because he was staying in a shed-sized bunkhouse. I have never suffered from anxiety or stress-related mental health challenges, so this experience was new and strange to me. Was it night terrors? I had heard of it but never experienced it personally. After weeks of this, here is a portion of my journal entry:

> *I don't remember ever feeling this alone. And so afraid. And I don't understand the pain in my body. I'm struggling to feel safe. I think I'm dying. I feel like I'm dying, and I don't want to be alone if I'm dying. How can this be happening?*

> *Is it because I'm alone for the first time in several decades? I'm sixty and can't be alone? And where's the physical pain coming from? So shitty! I feel encased in concrete when I try to move my body. Is it because I'm sixty? I should've treated my body better! Am I dying? Losing my mind? What the fuck?!!!!*

After further investigation and months spent delving into painful experiences that included processing unresolved past traumas, challenging beliefs about aging, learning how to regulate my nervous system to create more safety within myself, along with other fun activities, I am floating above the water's surface where the air is breathable again.

I am still learning more about the concept of being multidimensional and understanding that it is all about energy, that we are energetic beings here to experience the spectrum of frequencies in our day-to-day living and dying, that my vibrational frequency is the key to healing my body, and to moving toward or expanding into the new paradigm of connection and oneness.

Yes, I am a work in progress, as most of us are, but the scale of emotions has tipped in favor of the higher frequencies… most days. My experience during those recent months indicated strongly that I do not want to die when I am all alone. Fingers crossed that my plan is like Dad's.

Epilogue

Have you ever sat through a movie where the screen suddenly went dark, the credits started rolling, and you thought, "What the hell!?! That's it? That's how it ended?" We tend to find it unsatisfying without a hero's journey, happy ending, or a soothing *all is well and good*. As you may have noticed, the final chapter has no written summation as the rest did. And you may also be curious about why a book ended on the topic of death? Full disclosure, this chapter was already included in Book 2. Yes, we had earmarked it for a continuation of the new paradigm series. Before he died, Vince had also completed twenty-two more chapters of nonphysical messages from his guides for Book 2. In between edits and back and forth with one, we were preparing for full steam ahead on Book 2. As Mary and I regroup, we are committed to continuing to co-create, and to see the second book through to publication as well.

Now about death, it is not really an ending. I wanted to share why the new paradigm perception elevates the vibration to a higher frequency, rather than perceiving the circumstances as sullen, morose, dreadful, or depressing. These thoughts, emotions, and perceptions are low frequency, victim stance, something happening *to* us. In my experience with Vince's coaching and with his Trusted Source's guidance, every incident that feels devastating brings with it a perceivable gift, as well as the understanding that everything we choose to experience in life is a co-creation.

All of this was co-created with a soul whose choice included leaving the physical only hours after completing the last details of this book, and only days after completing twenty-two more chapters of guidance for Book 2. After the shock of Vince's death, it was time to perceive his passing as not a mistake, accident, or coincidence, and not right or wrong. Sad, of course, but purposefully, at some level, Vince *chose* a quick exit, early morning June 12, 2024, or it would not have occurred exactly as it had. He would explain it as his Higher Self, the higher frequency energy of his physical self "punching out." These were Vince's words to me when coaching on recognizing the wake-up calls that occur and acting on them, on living life consciously not unconsciously, and CHOOSING/DECIDING to reframe old belief systems and finally trusting that guidance comes from within. He was adamant about living fully, as planned, and when complete, we choose to return to the fullness of our vibration, the highest frequency of our energy stream, the ultimate "promotion."

The new paradigm holds a new perception of death. My very minimal understanding of quantum physics indicates scientifically that everything is energy, and since energy cannot be created or destroyed, living as energy beings in physical bodies, our conscious energetic selves continue after physical death.

Vince's death was yet another wake-up call for me personally. He stepped aside and left me and Mary to complete this project, to continue to share his work, sharing the new paradigm perspective of understanding and integrating. We are honored and committed to moving forward and completing Book 2, sharing the last powerful concepts intended for the world, on behalf of Vince from his Trusted Source, the highest vibration guidance that he trusted fully.

The last coaching with Vince helped me immensely in finally choosing the higher vibration of trusting my inner guidance and coming out the other side of doubt and needing certainty or to be right and feeling fear of being wrong. It was a day to remember. It finally clicked! Without the angel at the foot of my bed, I decided to choose to trust myself, my connection to constant inner guidance, to commit to consistency in practice, and to know when I align and am tuned in to nonphysical guidance, that I have plugged into home.

A Note from Mary

As I sit here reflecting on the journey that has brought us to this point, I am struck by the profound changes that have taken place, both within me and in the world Vince and I were building together. Vince's passing was a moment that shattered the ordinary, thrusting me into a new reality—one where his physical presence was no longer a part of my daily life. But in the midst of that loss, I found something unexpected: a deeper connection to the work we were doing, a more intimate understanding of the wisdom he imparted, and a renewed commitment to carry it forward.

It has been only eight weeks since Vince's passing, and yet the importance of moving this book to publication has never felt more urgent. In this short time, I am realizing that the work Vince left behind was just as much for me as it was for those ready to hear it now and in the decades to come. This new realization is slowly sinking in: What if my future depended on embodying his teachings just as much as it does for Michele? Who would I be without Vince in my life? And how would I live my Divine Intent on my path without the precious moments I had with him, and without the learned connection, guidance, and concepts?

The days following Vince's passing were filled with a mix of grief and an overwhelming sense of responsibility. I felt his absence keenly, but I also felt his presence in a different, more subtle way—guiding, encouraging, and reminding me of the importance of the path we had started on together. It wasn't long before I realized that this journey was far from over. In fact, it was just beginning, in a new form, with new challenges and new insights.

The work that Vince and I were doing was always about more than just the two of us. It was about a new way of seeing the world, a new paradigm of understanding our place in the Universe and the energy that connects us all. I am more determined than ever to continue this work, to bring the next book to life, and to share the messages that Vince was so passionate about.

In the chapters to come in Book 2, you will find a continuation of the journey we started—a deeper dive into the concepts that can transform how we see ourselves and the world around us. This is not just a book; it's an invitation to explore, to question, and to grow. It's a call to open your mind and your heart to the possibilities that lie beyond the physical, to the energy that continues to flow even after life as we know it has ended.

I hope you will join me on this next leg of the journey. The road ahead is filled with the same kind of wonder, discovery, and transformation that Vince and I sought to share from the beginning. And while his voice may no longer be here to guide us in person, his spirit and the wisdom he left behind are more than enough to light the way.

Thank you for being a part of this journey so far. I look forward to continuing it with you in the pages of our next book.

With gratitude and love,

Mary

About the Authors

Mary Kramer

Mary Kramer is a guide, teacher, and living example of the new paradigm concepts shared in this book. She has dedicated her life to integrating and *living* these teachings, demonstrating how self-awareness, conscious choice, and alignment with one's true nature create a life of purpose, meaning, and joy. As a mother, grandmother, and mentor, she inspires others to embrace their own transformation and step into the life they are meant to live.

Her late husband, Vince Kramer, was a visionary, pilot, and teacher devoted to guiding others toward their highest potential. The book you hold in your hands is his final work, completed the night before he passed. Through his channeled wisdom and Mary's lived experience, this book bridges spiritual insight with real-life application.

Together, their voices invite you to move beyond understanding these concepts and fully embody them.

Michele Ketzmerick

Michele Ketzmerick is a retired professional with a distinguished career in corrections and addiction treatment. Now residing in a peaceful, remote lake area of Saskatchewan, Canada, she has fully embraced her true passion—writing. Immersed in the serenity of nature, Michele draws inspiration from her surroundings and treasures the time spent with family, finding deep joy and fulfillment in creating enduring memories.

Retirement has been a transformative chapter, opening doors to personal growth, continued learning, and creative exploration. Michele is dedicated to expanding her knowledge and honing her craft, guided by a commitment to living with purpose and authenticity. Her journey has been profoundly influenced by the work of Vince and Mary Kramer, whose teachings on empowerment, self-discovery, and conscious living have played a pivotal role in both her writing endeavors and personal transformation.

Michele's path is a testament to the power of reinvention and the limitless possibilities that emerge when one follows their passions with curiosity and intention.

For more great books from Empower Press
Visit Books.GracePointPublishing.com

If you enjoyed reading *New Paradigm,* and purchased it through an online retailer, please return to the site and write a review to help others find the book.

www.ingramcontent.com/pod-product-compliance
Lightning Source LLC
Chambersburg PA
CBHW050550160426
43199CB00015B/2604